TapRooT®

Corrective Action Helper® Guide

SYSTEM IMPROVEMENTS, INC.
238 South Peters Road
Knoxville, Tennessee 37923-5224
(865) 539-2139 fax: (865) 539-4335
website: www.taproot.com
e-mail: info@taproot.com

Library of Congress
Cataloging-in-Publication Data
Paradies, Mark / Unger, Linda / Reed, Kenneth
TapRooT® Corrective Action Helper® Guide,
First Edition
p.   cm.
Aids in developing Corrective Actions when using the
TapRooT® Root Cause Analysis System.
ISBN   1-893130-05-3
1.   Business/Economics/Finance.
I. Paradies, Mark / Unger, Linda / Reed, Kenneth
II.   Type – Non-Fiction.

PRINTED IN THE UNITED STATES OF AMERICA

First Edition

Liability Disclaimer

The corrective action guidance provided in this book is NOT a complete and exhaustive list of all possible corrective actions. Rather, it is a starting point for the development of your corrective actions. Your judgment, experience, and knowledge are essential in the development of corrective actions. This Corrective Action Helper® Guide can't spot synergy between problems and corrective actions. You may be able to spot a single corrective action that solves multiple problems and is quite different from the individual corrective actions that you might develop by addressing each problem separately. You may decide that instead of trying to improve the system by implementing individual corrective actions, it might be better to re-engineer the entire system. This may include a complete redesign starting from scratch to remove Hazards or Targets. Once you have developed your corrective actions, we recommend that you have someone knowledgeable and independent from their development review them to evaluate their effectiveness and to evaluate them for potential unintended negative consequences. Therefore, because your knowledge, judgment, experience, and diligence and the knowledge, judgment, experience, and diligence of the reviewer are so important to the development of effective corrective actions, neither System Improvements nor any of its employees, contractors, or distributors take any responsibility for the corrective actions developed using this book. We provide no guarantee of the usefulness or effectiveness of the corrective actions that you develop. **THE ENTIRE RISK AS TO THE RESULTS AND PERFORMANCE OF THE CORRECTIVE ACTIONS IS ASSUMED BY YOU. IN NO EVENT SHALL SYSTEM IMPROVEMENTS OR ITS EMPLOYEES BE LIABLE TO YOU OR OTHERS FOR LOST PROFIT OR OTHER ECONOMIC LOSS, INDIRECT, SPECIAL CONSEQUENTIAL OR OTHER SIMILAR DAMAGES ARISING OUT OF YOUR USE OF THIS BOOK OR FOR ANY CLAIM MADE AGAINST YOU BY ANY OTHER PARTY EVEN IF SYSTEM IMPROVEMENTS HAS BEEN ADVISED OF THE POSSIBILITY OF SUCH CLAIM.** Finally, if the consequences of another incident of this type are unacceptable, you should recommend stopping activities/production or shutting down the facility until tested, effective corrective actions can be implemented.

TABLE OF CONTENTS

USING THE CORRECTIVE ACTION HELPER® GUIDE

This aid is for developing useful, effective, complete corrective actions after identifying their Root Causes using the Root Cause Tree®. Each Root Cause in the Root Cause Tree® has an associated *Corrective Action Helper® Guide* entry. Each entry is divided into 4 parts:

1. **Check:** Do you agree that the Root Cause you are trying to fix actually applies to the problem?

2. **Ideas to help fix the Root Cause:** The *Corrective Action Helper® Guide* suggests ways to correct the Specific Root Cause. Not only does it make you think of the obvious answers; it helps you think outside the box – beyond your area of expertise or comfort.

3. **Ideas for Generic Cause(s):** It reminds the investigator to look for Generic Root Causes and suggests ways to fix the generic issues.

4. **Reference:** It provides references for more detailed, in-depth research into ways to improve performance. Even if you are not an expert in a particular area, this further reading helps you discover ways to fix the problem.

The *Corrective Action Helper® Guide* doesn't provide the fixes; rather, it provides ideas. These entries give you a start to develop effective methods to improve performance. We hope this book gets your creative juices flowing. When used in conjunction with the SMARTER Matrix, Root Causes will be fixed by corrective actions that are much more effective than your previous improvement efforts.

To simplify the text, instead of referring to Causal Factors or issues, we will call all problems "issues."

To find an entry for a category on the Root Cause Tree®, simply look for the name of the Basic Cause Category and Near Root Cause Category in the block at the edge of each page or look in the Table of Contents.

The *Corrective Action Helper® Guide* is part of the TapRooT® System for root cause analysis and performance improvement. For details, see the *TapRooT® Book*, (2008). To order the book, see:

www.taproot.com

or call System Improvements in the United States at:

865-539-2139

Level 1: Top of the Tree

Check: You have decided that this problem was caused by a Human Performance Difficulty but you have not progressed down the Root Cause Tree® to the Root Cause level.

Ideas:

- Effective corrective action based on Root cause analysis is not possible unless you progress further down the Root Cause Tree®.

- If you cannot progress further down the tree, then consider performing a Safeguards Analysis (Chapter 10 of the *TapRooT® Book*, 2008) to identify potential Safeguards that you could add to reduce the likelihood of this incident recurring.

References:

- *What Went Wrong?* (1998), by Trevor A. Kletz, published by Gulf Professional Publishing.

- *Handbook of Human Performance Technology, 3rd Edition,* (2006) by James Pershing, published by Pfeiffer.

- *Human Performance Improvement, Second Edition: Building Practitioner Competence,* (2007) by William Rothwell, published by Butterworth-Heinemann.

- *Human Performance Measures Handbook,* (2000) by Valerie Jane Gawron, published by CRC.

Check: You have decided that this problem was caused by an Equipment Difficulty but you have not progressed down the Root Cause Tree® to the Root Cause level.

Ideas:

- Effective corrective action based on Root cause analysis is not possible unless you progress further down the Root Cause Tree®.

- If you cannot progress further down the tree after performing an Equifactor® Analysis, then consider performing a Safeguards Analysis (Chapter 10 of the *TapRooT® Book,* 2008) to identify potential Safeguards that you could add to reduce the likelihood of this incident recurring.

- Consider performing a Change Analysis to help troubleshoot the equipment problem.

References:

- For more information on performing an Equifactor® Analysis, attend an Equifactor® Course. For information call (865) 539-2139.

- *Machinery Failure Analysis & Troubleshooting, Volume 2,* (1983) by Heinz Bloch & Fred Geitner, published by Gulf Publishing Company, Houston, TX.

- *Improving Machinery Reliability,* (1988) by Heinz Bloch, published by Gulf Publishing Company, Houston, TX.

- *What Went Wrong?* (1998) by Trevor A. Kletz, published by Gulf Professional Publishing.

- *Electrical Equipment Handbook: Troubleshooting and Maintenance,* (2003) by Philip Kiameh, published by McGraw-Hill Professional.

- *A Working Guide to Process Equipment,* (2002) by Norman and Elizabeth Lieberman, published by McGraw-Hill Professional.

- *Industrial Machinery Repair: Best Maintenance Practices Pocket Guide,* (2003) by Ricky Smith, published by Butterworth-Heinemann.

Check: You have decided that this problem was caused by a Natural Disaster or Sabotage.

Ideas:

- Consider performing a Safeguards Analysis (Chapter 10 of the *TapRooT® Book,* 2008) to identify potential Safeguards that you could add to reduce the likelihood of sabotage or natural phenomenon from causing a similar incident in the future.

- For cases of sabotage you may consider providing your information to the proper authorities for a criminal investigation.

References:

- *Insider Threat: Protecting the Enterprise from Sabotage, Spying, and Theft,* (2005) by Eric Cole and Sandra Ring, published by Syngress.

- *Effective Physical Security, Third Edition,* (2003) by Lawrence Fennelly, published by Butterworth-Heinemann.

- *Computer Security Handbook,* (2002) by Seymour Bosworth and Michel Kabay, published by Wiley.

- *Security, ID Systems, and Locks: The Book on Electronic Access Control,* (1997) by Joel Konicek and Karen Little, published by Butterworth-Heinemann.

OTHER (SPECIFY)

Check: You have decided that the cause of this problem is not covered by the Root Cause Tree® or the information you have is insufficient to perform Root cause analysis.

Ideas:

- Effective corrective action based on Root cause analysis is not possible unless you progress further down the Root Cause Tree®.

- If you cannot progress further down the tree, then consider performing a Safeguards Analysis (Chapter 10 of the *TapRooT® Book*, 2008) to identify potential Safeguards that you could add to reduce the likelihood of this incident recurring.

- If this cause of the problem is not covered by the tree, record as much information as you can and develop corrective actions based on your judgment. Contact System Improvements at (865) 539-2139 to report the new cause that you have discovered.

- If you could not progress down the tree due to lack of information, consider adding additional systems to record more information in future incidents so that your analysis can more effectively pinpoint the Root Causes. Video and voice recording, as well as data recorders, should be considered.

LEVELS 1 – 5: Equipment Difficulty

TOLERABLE FAILURE

Check: You have decided that this is a random equipment failure that is difficult to predict and not worth fixing.

Ideas:

- You have decided that this equipment problem is NOT worth fixing. Therefore, no corrective action is recommended beyond replacing the failed equipment.

- However, you should keep a list of unexpected failures that have been approved by respected technical personnel. This will improve the consistency of analysis of unexpected failures and will help you track the failure rate so that you can detect repeat failures.

DESIGN

Check: You have decided that the design of the equipment needs to be improved to prevent future equipment failures.

Ideas:

- You should continue to analyze the cause of this problem to find the Root Cause of the design problem.

- You will then consider redesigning the equipment or conducting a Safeguards Analysis (Chapter 10 of the *TapRooT® Book*, 2008) to identify potential Safeguards that you could add to reduce the likelihood of this equipment failure.

References:

- Code of Federal Regulations (Pharmaceuticals) 21CFR211 Subpart D, *Equipment*.

- Australian Safety Standard AS 4024.1 -2006 Series - *Safety of Machinery*, www.saiglobal.com/shop/Script/Details.asp?DocN=AS929870415561.

- *Medical Device and Equipment Design: Usability Engineering and Ergonomics*, (1995) by Michael E. Wiklund, published by CRC.

- *Chemical Process Equipment, Second Edition: Selection and Design*, (2000) by James Couper et al., published by Gulf Professional Publishing.

- *Medical and Dental Space Planning: A Comprehensive Guide to Design, Equipment, and Clinical Procedures*, (2002) by Jain Malkin, published by Wiley.

- *Mechanical and Electrical Equipment for Buildings, 10th Edition*, (2005) by Benjamin Stein et al, published by Wiley.

- *Ludwig's Applied Process Design for Chemical and Petrochemical Plants, Volume 1, Fourth Edition*, (2007) by Ernest E. Ludwig, published by Gulf Professional Publishing.

DESIGN SPECS **Check:** You have decided that the design of the equipment should be improved to prevent future equipment failures.

Ideas:

This problem has two areas that need to be considered. First, the problem with the design and, second, the problem with the design process.

- First, you should consider recommending redesign of the equipment to eliminate the problem introduced by the design specification deficiency.

- Second, you should continue to analyze the cause of this problem to find the Root Cause of the design specification problem. One idea might be to consider changing the guidance given to engineers who develop design specifications.

Ideas for Generic Problems:

- If there is a generic problem, you should consider changing the design process or the training for engineers to reduce the likelihood of engineers making this type of design error in the future.

References:

- Code of Federal Regulations (Pharmaceuticals) 21CFR211 Subpart D, *Equipment*.

- Australian Safety Standard AS 4024.1 - 2006 Series - *Safety of Machinery*, www.saiglobal.com/shop/Script/Details.asp?DocN=AS929870415561.

- *Medical Device and Equipment Design: Usability Engineering and Ergonomics*, (1995) by Michael E. Wiklund, published by CRC.

- *Chemical Process Equipment, Second Edition: Selection and Design*, (2000) by James Couper et al., published by Gulf Professional Publishing.

- *Medical and Dental Space Planning: A Comprehensive Guide to Design, Equipment, and Clinical Procedures*, (2002) by Jain Malkin, published by Wiley.

- *Mechanical and Electrical Equipment for Buildings, 10th Edition*, (2005) by Benjamin Stein et al, published by Wiley.

- *Ludwig's Applied Process Design for Chemical and Petrochemical Plants, Volume 1, Fourth Edition*, (2007) by Ernest E. Ludwig, published by Gulf Professional Publishing.

- *Supply of Machinery Safety Regulations*, (1992) United Kingdom.

- *Machinery Directive 98/37/EC*, (1998) European Union.

- *Equipment intended for use in Potentially Explosive Atmospheres*, (May 2007), ATEX 94/9/EC, European Union.

Specs NI **Check:** You have found that the design specifications for this equipment need improvement.

Ideas:

This problem has two areas that need to be considered. First, the problem with the design and, second, the problem with the design process.

- First, you should consider recommending redesign of the equipment to eliminate the problem introduced by the design specification deficiency.

- Second, you should continue to analyze the cause of this problem to find the Root Cause of the design specification problem. One idea might be to consider changing the guidance given to engineers who develop design specifications.

Ideas for Generic Problems:

- If there is a generic problem, you should consider changing the design process or the training for engineers to reduce the likelihood of engineers making this type of design error in the future.

References:

- Code of Federal Regulations (Pharmaceuticals) 21CFR211 Subpart D, *Equipment.*

- Australian Safety Standard AS 4024.1 -2006 Series - *Safety of Machinery,* www.saiglobal.com/shop/Script/Details.asp?DocN=AS929870415561.

- *Medical Device and Equipment Design: Usability Engineering and Ergonomics,* (1995) by Michael E. Wiklund, published by CRC.

- *Chemical Process Equipment, Second Edition: Selection and Design,* (2000) by James Couper et al., published by Gulf Professional Publishing.

- *Medical and Dental Space Planning: A Comprehensive Guide to Design, Equipment, and Clinical Procedures,* (2002) by Jain Malkin, published by Wiley.

- *Mechanical and Electrical Equipment for Buildings, 10th Edition,* (2005) by Benjamin Stein et al, published by Wiley.

- *Ludwig's Applied Process Design for Chemical and Petrochemical Plants, Volume 1, Fourth Edition,* (2007) by Ernest E. Ludwig, published by Gulf Professional Publishing.

Check: You have decided that the design specifications were OK, but the design did not meet the specifications.

Ideas:

- Consider recommending an improved design that meets the specs.
- Consider the Root Causes of the design not meeting the specs.

Ideas for Generic Problems:

- If there is a generic problem, you should consider recommending ways to improve the design process, design review, or designer training to reduce the likelihood that designers will make the same type of mistake in the future.

References:

- Code of Federal Regulations (Pharmaceuticals) 21CFR211 Subpart D, *Equipment.*

- Australian Safety Standard AS 4024.1 -2006 Series - *Safety of Machinery,* www.saiglobal.com/shop/Script/Details.asp?DocN=AS929870415561.

- *Medical Device and Equipment Design: Usability Engineering and Ergonomics,* (1995) by Michael E. Wiklund, published by CRC.

- *Chemical Process Equipment, Second Edition: Selection and Design,* (2000) by James Couper et al., published by Gulf Professional Publishing.

- *Medical and Dental Space Planning: A Comprehensive Guide to Design, Equipment, and Clinical Procedures,* (2002) by Jain Malkin, published by Wiley.

- *Mechanical and Electrical Equipment for Buildings, 10th Edition,* (2005) by Benjamin Stein et al, published by Wiley.

- *Ludwig's Applied Process Design for Chemical and Petrochemical Plants, Volume 1, Fourth Edition,* (2007) by Ernest E. Ludwig, published by Gulf Professional Publishing.

Problem Not Anticipated

Check: You have decided that the design needed improvement because the designer did not anticipate a problem that should have been anticipated.

Ideas:

- Consider recommending an improved design that eliminates the problem that was not anticipated.

- Consider further investigation to determine the Root Causes of the reason that the designer did not anticipate the problem and the design reviewer did not detect the problem.

Ideas for Generic Problems:

- You should try to identify the Generic Cause of the designer not recognizing the problem and consider recommending ways to improve the design process, design review, or training of the designer to reduce the likelihood that designers will make the same type of mistake in the future.

References:

- Code of Federal Regulations (Pharmaceuticals) 21CFR211 Subpart D, *Equipment.*

- Australian Safety Standard AS 4024.1 -2006 Series - *Safety of Machinery,* www.saiglobal.com/shop/Script/Details.asp?DocN=AS929870415561.

- *Medical Device and Equipment Design: Usability Engineering and Ergonomics,* (1995) by Michael E. Wiklund, published by CRC.

- *Chemical Process Equipment, Second Edition: Selection and Design,* (2000) by James Couper et al., published by Gulf Professional Publishing.

- *Medical and Dental Space Planning: A Comprehensive Guide to Design, Equipment, and Clinical Procedures,* (2002) by Jain Malkin, published by Wiley.

- *Mechanical and Electrical Equipment for Buildings, 10th Edition,* (2005) by Benjamin Stein et al, published by Wiley.

- *Ludwig's Applied Process Design for Chemical and Petrochemical Plants, Volume 1, Fourth Edition,* (2007) by Ernest E. Ludwig, published by Gulf Professional Publishing.

equipment environment not considered:

Check: You have decided that the design needed improvement because the designer did not anticipate a problem with the equipment's operating environment that should have been anticipated.

Ideas:

- You should consider either recommending an improved design that will work in the intended equipment environment or modifying the equipment environment to make the environment acceptable for the existing equipment.

- Consider further investigation to determine the Root Causes of the reason that the designer did not anticipate the problem and the design reviewer did not detect the problem.

Ideas for Generic Problems:

- You should try to identify the Generic Cause of the designer not considering the equipment's environment when designing the equipment and consider recommending ways to improve the design process, design review, or training of the designer to reduce the likelihood that designers will make the same type of mistake in the future.

References:

- Code of Federal Regulations (Pharmaceuticals) 21CFR211 Subpart D, *Equipment.*

- Australian Safety Standard AS 4024.1 -2006 Series - *Safety of Machinery,* www.saiglobal.com/shop/Script/Details.asp?DocN=AS929870415561.

- *Medical Device and Equipment Design: Usability Engineering and Ergonomics,* (1995) by Michael E. Wiklund, published by CRC.

- *Chemical Process Equipment, Second Edition: Selection and Design,* (2000) by James Couper et al., published by Gulf Professional Publishing.

- *Medical and Dental Space Planning: A Comprehensive Guide to Design, Equipment, and Clinical Procedures,* (2002) by Jain Malkin, published by Wiley.

- *Mechanical and Electrical Equipment for Buildings, 10th Edition,* (2005) by Benjamin Stein et al, published by Wiley.

- *Ludwig's Applied Process Design for Chemical and Petrochemical Plants, Volume 1, Fourth Edition,* (2007) by Ernest E. Ludwig, published by Gulf Professional Publishing.

DESIGN REVIEW Check: You have decided that the equipment failure was at least partially caused by the design reviewer not detecting a problem that he should have been expected to detect.

Ideas:

- Consider recommending an improved design that eliminates the problem that was overlooked in the design review.

- Consider analyzing the Root Cause of the failure of the design review.

Ideas for Generic Problems:

- If you identify a Generic Cause of the design reviewer not identifying the problem with the design, consider recommending ways to improve the design review process, the Management of Change process, or training the design reviewer to reduce the likelihood that the reviewer will make the same type of mistake in the future.

References:

- Code of Federal Regulations (Pharmaceuticals) 21CFR211 Subpart D, *Equipment.*

- Australian Safety Standard AS 4024.1 -2006 Series - *Safety of Machinery,* www.saiglobal.com/shop/Script/Details.asp?DocN=AS929870415561.

- *Medical Device and Equipment Design: Usability Engineering and Ergonomics,* (1995) by Michael E. Wiklund, published by CRC.

- *Chemical Process Equipment, Second Edition: Selection and Design,* (2000) by James Couper et al., published by Gulf Professional Publishing.

- *Medical and Dental Space Planning: A Comprehensive Guide to Design, Equipment, and Clinical Procedures,* (2002) by Jain Malkin, published by Wiley.

- *Mechanical and Electrical Equipment for Buildings, 10th Edition,* (2005) by Benjamin Stein et al, published by Wiley.

- *Ludwig's Applied Process Design for Chemical and Petrochemical Plants, Volume 1, Fourth Edition,* (2007) by Ernest E. Ludwig, published by Gulf Professional Publishing.

Independent Review NI

Check: You have decided that the equipment failure was at least partially caused by the design review not detecting a problem that should have been detected. Also, the reason the design review didn't catch the problem was the reviewer was not independent of the original design.

Ideas:

- You should consider recommending an improved design that eliminates the problem that was overlooked in the design review.

Ideas for Generic Problems:

- If non-independent design review is a generic problem, consider recommending changes in the process to improve the independence of the design reviewer in the design review process.

References:

- Code of Federal Regulations (Pharmaceuticals) 21CFR211 Subpart D, *Equipment*.

- Australian Safety Standard AS 4024.1 -2006 Series - *Safety of Machinery*, www.saiglobal.com/shop/Script/Details.asp?DocN=AS929870415561.

- *Medical Device and Equipment Design: Usability Engineering and Ergonomics*, (1995) by Michael E. Wiklund, published by CRC.

- *Chemical Process Equipment, Second Edition: Selection and Design*, (2000) by James Couper et al., published by Gulf Professional Publishing.

- *Medical and Dental Space Planning: A Comprehensive Guide to Design, Equipment, and Clinical Procedures*, (2002) by Jain Malkin, published by Wiley.

- *Mechanical and Electrical Equipment for Buildings, 10th Edition*, (2005) by Benjamin Stein et al, published by Wiley.

- *Ludwig's Applied Process Design for Chemical and Petrochemical Plants, Volume 1, Fourth Edition*, (2007) by Ernest E. Ludwig, published by Gulf Professional Publishing.

management of change (MOC) NI:

Check: You have decided that an independent review of the design change (Management of Change or 50.59 review) would have detected the problem with the design modification and thereby would have prevented the problem.

Ideas:

- If there was no adequate policy for a Management of Change review, consider recommending a policy and training the workforce on the requirements for Management of Change.

- If there was a policy but it wasn't used, consider the corrective actions under Management System - SPAC Not Used.

- If the Management of Change policy was not used because the supervisor or workers did not understand the policy, consider corrective actions under the Training Basic Cause Category.

- If there are repeated failures to use the Management of Change policy, consider the ideas for generic problems in the next section.

Ideas for Generic Problems:

- Consider recommending the evaluation your Management of Change program to determine the reasons that the program is not working. This evaluation could start with an audit of the Management of Change program and a root cause analysis of the issues uncovered.

- Once you have corrected the problems with your Management of Change program, you should consider conducting training for all affected personnel.

- To ensure that the changes you are implementing are adequate and continue to be properly applied, consider implementing a continuing periodic audit of the Management of Change program.

References:

- OSHA 29CFR1910.119 Process Safety Management of Highly Hazardous Chemicals, section 1910.119(l), Management of Change (http://www.osha.gov/pls/oshaweb/owadisp.show_document?p_table=STANDARDS&p_id=9760).

- The Center for Chemical Process Safety has numerous references with detailed ideas on how to improve your Management of Change process. See http://www.aiche.org/CCPS/index.aspx.

hazard analysis NI:

Check: You have decided that a Hazard Analysis of the design would have detected the problem with the design and thereby would have prevented the problem.

Ideas:

- If there was no adequate policy for conducting a Hazard Analysis, consider recommending a policy and training the applicable members of the workforce on the requirements for Hazard Analysis.

- If there was a policy that required a Hazard Analysis but it wasn't performed, consider the corrective actions under the Management System - SPAC Not Used.

- If the policy requiring Hazard Analysis was not used because the people responsible did not understand the policy, consider corrective actions under the Training Basic Cause Category.

- If there are repeated failures to analyze hazards, consider the ideas for generic problems in the next section.

Ideas for Generic Problems:

- Consider evaluating the design and Hazard Analysis process to determine the reasons that the process failed. This evaluation could start with an audit of the design and Hazard Analysis process and a Root cause analysis of any issues uncovered.

- Once you have corrected the problems with your design and Hazard Analysis program, consider conducting training for all affected personnel.

- To ensure that the changes you are implementing are adequate and continue to be properly applied, consider implementing a continuing periodic audit of the design and Hazard Analysis process.

References:

- *Hazard Identification and Risk Assessment by Geoff Wells* (1996), ISBN 978-0852954638.

- *Guidelines for Hazard Evaluation Procedures, 2nd Edition with Worked Examples,* (1992) Center for Chemical Process Safety, New York, ISBN 978-0816904914.

- *Guidelines for Chemical Process Quantitative Risk Analysis,* (2000) 2nd Edition, Center for Chemical Process Safety, New York, ISBN 978-0816907205.

- *Human Reliability & Safety Analysis Data Handbook,* (1994) David Gertman and Harold Blackman, John Wiley & Sons, New York,

Check: You have decided that the equipment difficulty was caused by a defective part or piece of equipment.

Ideas:

- Continue analyzing the Root Cause of this problem. Then consider conducting a Safeguards Analysis (Chapter 10 of the *TapRooT® Book,*

2008) to identify potential Safeguards that you could add to reduce the likelihood of this equipment or part failing, or conducting an Equifactor® Analysis.

- If you can't find the cause of the equipment or part failing, you may want to consider redesigning the equipment or process to eliminate the defective part.

- Statistical Process Control (SPC) may be helpful in analyzing the causes of equipment/parts defective and in developing corrective actions. For more information about SPC, read Understanding Statistical Process Control (Authors: Donald J. Wheeler and David S. Chambers, Published by: SPC Press, Knoxville, TN).

- Change Analysis (Chapter 11 of the TapRooT® Book, 2008) may also be helpful if this part or equipment has a long history of successful performance but has started to fail frequently.

Ideas for Generic Problems:

- If you find that this is a generic problem, consider implementing a programmatic fix that ensures that other parts or equipment won't be defective in the future. This could start with a review of how parts are purchased, handled, stored, and checked.

PROCUREMENT **Check:** You have decided that defective or improper parts or equipment were obtained from a vendor because of problems in the procurement process.

Ideas:

- Consider replacing the defective part with one that is not defective. (Careful! If you get a new part through the same procurement process, the new part may also be defective. Consider pre-installation testing to ensure that the part works as designed.)

- Consider finding the Root Cause(s) of the procurement problems by creating a new SnapCharT® for procurement of the defective part and identifying the Causal Factors that need further analysis to discover the procurement problem's Root Cause(s).

Ideas for Generic Problems:

- If you find that parts procurement is a generic problem, you should consider recommending a review of the entire procurement process that could include benchmarking your procurement processes against other facilities with a reputation for highly reliable performance. The goal of the review would be to identify programmatic fixes that would ensure better purchasing performance in the future.

References:

- *Purchasing Capital Equipment,* (1998) by John Mahoney, published by PT Publications Inc.

- *Lean Supply Chain Management: A Handbook for Strategic Procurement,* (2003) by Jeffrey Wincel, published by Productivity Press.

- *The Procurement and Supply Manager's Desk reference,* (2007) by Fred Sollish and John Semanik, published by Wiley.

- *Purchasing: Selection and Procurement for the Hospitality Industry,* (2007) by Andrew Feinstein and John Stefanelli, published by Wiley.

- *E-Procurement: From Strategy to Implementation,* (2001) by Dale Neef, published by FT Press.

MANUFACTURING **Check:** You have decided that parts or equipment were defective when obtained from the manufacturer.

Ideas:

- Consider replacing the defective part. (Careful! If you get a new part from the same manufacturer or from the same manufacturing process, the new part may also be defective. Consider pre-installation testing to ensure that the part works as designed.)

- Next, if you want to ensure that the manufacturer improves their process, get them to analyze the Root Causes of their manufacturing difficulties using TapRooT®.

- If they aren't familiar with TapRooT®, recommend that they attend a TapRooT® Course. For the current schedule, call (865) 539-2139 or see www.taproot.com.

HANDLING **Check:** You have decided that the parts or equipment were damaged during handling before installation but after they were manufactured.

Ideas:

- Consider replacing the defective part. (Careful! If the new part is handled the same way as the old one, the new part may also be defective. Consider specifying handling procedures and pre-installation testing to ensure that the new part works as needed.)

- Next, to identify the Root Causes of these handling problems, draw a SnapCharT® for the handling of the defective part, identify the Causal Factors, and find their Root Causes.

Equipment Difficulty

Ideas for Generic Problems:

- If you find that handling of parts and equipment is a generic problem, consider recommending a review of how parts are handled that could include benchmarking your handling processes and procedures against other facilities with a reputation for highly reliable performance. The goal of the review would be to identify programmatic fixes that would ensure better handling of parts in the future.

References:

- *Tool and Manufacturing Engineers Handbook Vol 9: Material and Part Handling,* (1998) by Philip Mitchell, published by the Society of Manufacturing Engineers.

STORAGE **Check:** You have decided that parts or equipment were damaged during storage before installation (including parts that were issued past their storage shelf lives).

Ideas:

- Consider replacing the defective part. (Careful! If you get a new part from the same storage facility, the new part may also be defective. Consider ordering a fresh part that has not been stored and/or pre-installation testing to ensure that the part works as needed.)

- Next, to identify the Root Causes of the storage problem, draw a SnapCharT® for the storage of the part, identify the Causal Factors, and find their Root Causes.

Ideas for Generic Problems:

- If you find that storage of parts and equipment is a generic problem, consider recommending a review of how parts are stored. This review could include benchmarking your storage against other facilities with a reputation for highly reliable performance. The goal of the review would be to identify programmatic fixes that would ensure better storage of parts in the future.

References:

- *Analysis and Algorithms for Service Parts Supply Chains,* (2004) by John Muckstadt, published by Springer.

QUALITY CONTROL **Check:** You have decided that the problem was at least partially caused by the failure to perform reasonable inspections, functional tests, or quality verification checks during or after completion of work or because the checks that were performed failed to detect the problem when a reasonable check should have caught it.

Ideas:

- You should continue to analyze this problem until you find a Root Cause. You can then correct the Root Causes.

- If you can't identify the Root Causes, then perform a Safeguards Analysis (Chapter 10 of the *TapRooT® Book,* 2008) to identify potential Safeguards that could reduce the likelihood of this problem recurring.

- Also, consider recommending improved inspections, functional tests, or quality verifications even if you don't know the Root Cause of this problem.

- Be careful that you don't try to use inspections to fix every problem. Instead, you may want to consider other methods to improve quality such as Statistical Process Control (SPC) or re-engineering the work to eliminate the potential for this kind of problem.

- To start re-engineering the process, first develop a detailed SnapCharT® of the current process to help optimize the process. See Chapter 4 and Chapter 7 of the *TapRooT® Book,* (2008).

- You may also perform a Safeguards Analysis (Chapter 10 of the *TapRooT® Book,* 2008) to identify potential Safeguards that you could add to reduce the likelihood of this problem recurring without requiring an additional QC check.

Ideas for Generic Problems:

- If you decide that QC is a generic problem, then you should consider recommending corrective actions to eliminate the cause. These corrective actions would depend on the Root Causes that you identify.

- One way to start the improvement process for a generic QC problem is to benchmark your QC practices against other facilities with a reputation for highly reliable performance. The goal of the review would be to identify programmatic fixes that would improve your QC process and lead to improved overall performance.

- Also, you should consider recommending a review of similar work so that other similar work can be improved before a similar, but different, incident occurs.

- If the effort to review the work is extensive because of the number or complexity of the tasks, consider recommending a phased approach by prioritizing the work to be reviewed and addressing the most important tasks first.

References:

- For more information about SPC, read: *Understanding Statistical Process Control,* (1992) by Donald J. Wheeler and David S. Chambers and published by SPC Press, Knoxville, TN.

- Code of Federal Regulations (Pharmaceuticals) 21CFR211.22, *Responsibilities of Quality Control Unit.*

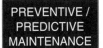

PREVENTIVE / PREDICTIVE MAINTENANCE

Check: Your analysis has indicated a problem with the equipment's preventive or predictive maintenance program.

Ideas:

- Effective corrective action based on Root cause analysis would be easier if you progress further down the Root Cause Tree®.

- If you cannot progress further down the tree, then consider performing a Safeguards Analysis (Chapter 10 of the *TapRooT® Book,* 2008) to identify potential Safeguards that you could add to reduce the likelihood of this incident recurring.

- Also consider installing recording equipment to record more information about future equipment failures so that you could better analyze the Root Causes of the failure and develop improved PMs.

References:

- *Reliability-centred Maintenance,* (2001) by John Moubray, published by Butterworth-Heinemann.

- *Reliability-centered Maintenance,* (1978) by F.S. Nowlan and H. Heape, published by National Technical Information Service, Springfield, VA.

- *Demonstration of Reliability Centered Maintenance,* (1991) by J.P. Gaertner, published by Electric Power Research Institute, Palo Alto, CA.

- *Maintenance Engineering Handbook,* (2001) Authors: Various, published by McGraw-Hill, New York.

- *Preventive Maintenance Good Practice:* Institute of Nuclear Power Operations, Atlanta, GA.

- *Maintenance Management for Medical Equipment* (ASHE).

PM NI

Check: Your analysis has indicated a problem with the equipment's preventive or predictive maintenance program.

Ideas:

- Effective corrective action based on Root cause analysis would be easier if you progress further down the Root Cause Tree®.

- If you cannot progress further down the tree, then consider performing a Safeguards Analysis (Chapter 10 of the *TapRooT® Book,* 2008) to identify potential Safeguards that you could add to reduce the likelihood of this incident recurring.

- Consider conducting a proactive Equifactor® Analysis to identify areas that may need PMs. See Chapter 9 of the *TapRooT® Book,* (2008).

- If you had trouble finding a Root Cause because the maintenance records and preventive maintenance documentation were unavailable, incomplete, or inaccurate and prevented you from analyzing the problem, consider recommending improvements to the documentation system.

- Also consider installing recording equipment to record more information about future equipment failures so that you could better analyze the Root Causes of the failure.

- Once you have developed the improved preventive/predictive maintenance program for the particular equipment involved, consider providing training for the technicians, mechanics, schedulers, operators, supervisors, and managers who will be performing and supervising the maintenance.

Ideas for Generic Problems:

- Consider recommending a review of equipment preventive or predictive maintenance for critical or safety significant equipment.

- Next use the information from the review to recommend PM improvements for all equipment that needs improved maintenance.

- Once you have developed the improved preventive/predictive maintenance program for the particular equipment involved, consider providing training for the technicians, mechanics, schedulers, operators, supervisors, and managers who will be performing and supervising the maintenance.

References:

- *Reliability-centered Maintenance,* (2001) by F.S. Nowlan and H. Heap, Publisher: National Technical Information Service, Springfield, VA.

- *Reliability-centred Maintenance* by John Moubray, published by Butterworth-Heinemann.

- *Demonstration of Reliability Centered Maintenance,* (1991) by J.P. Gaertner, Publisher: Electric Power Research Institute, Palo Alto, CA.

- *Maintenance Engineering Handbook,* (2001) Authors: Various, Publisher: McGraw-Hill, New York.
- *Preventive Maintenance Good Practice*: Institute of Nuclear Power Operations, Atlanta, GA.
- *Maintenance Management for Medical Equipment* (ASHE).

No PM for Equip

Check: Your analysis has shown that there was no PM for the equipment when, in your judgment, there should have been PM to reduce the likelihood of this type of equipment failure.

Ideas:

- Consider developing a preventive or predictive maintenance program for the equipment.

- To get ideas to develop this improved program, review industry best practices, ask for vendor recommendations, and review industry failure databases to develop preventive maintenance intervals.

- Consider conducting a proactive Equifactor® Analysis to identify areas that may need PMs. See Chapter 9 of the *TapRooT® Book,* (2008).

- Once you have developed the improved preventive/predictive maintenance program for the particular equipment involved, consider providing training for the technicians, mechanics, schedulers, operators, supervisors, and managers who will be performing and supervising the maintenance.

Ideas for Generic Problems:

If you find that a lack of preventive or predictive maintenance is a generic problem:

- Consider recommending a review of equipment preventive or predictive maintenance for critical or safety significant equipment.

- Next use the information from the review to recommend PM improvements for all equipment that needs improved maintenance.

- Consider conducting a proactive Equifactor® Analysis to identify areas that may need PMs. See Chapter 9 of the *TapRooT® Book,* (2008).

- Once you have developed the improved preventive/predictive maintenance program for the particular equipment involved, consider providing training for the technicians, mechanics, schedulers, operators, supervisors, and managers who will be performing and supervising the maintenance.

References:

- *Reliability-centered Maintenance,* (2001) by F.S. Nowlan and H. Heap, Publisher: National Technical Information Service, Springfield, VA.

- *Reliability-centred Maintenance* by John Moubray, published by Butterworth-Heinemann.

- *Demonstration of Reliability Centered Maintenance,* (1991) by J.P. Gaertner, Publisher: Electric Power Research Institute, Palo Alto, CA.

- *Maintenance Engineering Handbook,* (2001) Authors: Various, Publisher: McGraw-Hill, New York.

- *Preventive Maintenance Good Practice:* Institute of Nuclear Power Operations, Atlanta, GA.

- *Maintenance Management for Medical Equipment* (ASHE).

PM for Equip NI

Check: You have decided that the PM for the equipment needs improvement.

Ideas:

- Consider improving the preventive or predictive maintenance program for the equipment. To get ideas to develop this improved program:
- Review industry best practices.
- Ask for vendor recommendations.
- Review industry failure databases to develop preventive maintenance intervals.
- Once you have developed the improved preventive/predictive maintenance program for the particular equipment involved, consider providing training for the technicians, mechanics, schedulers, operators, supervisors, and managers who will be performing and supervising the maintenance.

Ideas for Generic Problems:

- If you find that preventive or predictive maintenance needing improvement is a generic problem, consider recommending a review of equipment preventive or predictive maintenance for critical or safety significant equipment.

- You would then recommend improved PM for all equipment that needs better maintenance.

- Once you have developed the improved preventive/predictive maintenance program for the particular equipment involved, consider providing training for the technicians, mechanics, schedulers, operators, supervisors, and managers who will be performing and supervising the maintenance.

References:

- *Reliability-centered Maintenance,* (2001) by F.S. Nowlan and H. Heap, Publisher: National Technical Information Service, Springfield, VA.

- *Reliability-centred Maintenance* by John Moubray, published by Butterworth-Heinemann.

- *Demonstration of Reliability Centered Maintenance,* (1991) by J.P. Gaertner, Publisher: Electric Power Research Institute, Palo Alto, CA.

- *Maintenance Engineering Handbook,* (2001) Authors: Various, Publisher: McGraw-Hill, New York.

- *Preventive Maintenance Good Practice:* Institute of Nuclear Power Operations, Atlanta, GA.

- *Maintenance Management for Medical Equipment* (ASHE).

REPEAT FAILURE **Check:** You have decided that this failure rate is too frequent for the intended purpose of this equipment.

Ideas:

- Repeat failures indicate that some other category or categories are causing the equipment to fail over and over again. Consider troubleshooting the failure using Equifactor®.

- You should continue to analyze other equipment difficulty areas of the Root Cause Tree® to find the Root Causes.

- If you cannot find any Root Causes, then you should consider conducting a Safeguards Analysis (Chapter 10 of the *TapRooT® Book,* 2008) to identify potential Safeguards that you could add to reduce the likelihood of this incident recurring.

- You may consider redesigning the equipment or process that is causing the repeat failures.

- Statistical Process Control (SPC) may be helpful in analyzing the causes of repeat failures and in developing corrective actions. For more information about SPC, read *Understanding Statistical Process Control* (Authors: Donald J. Wheeler and David S. Chambers, Published by: SPC Press, Knoxville, TN).

- Also, you should keep a list of repeat failures that have been identified in previous incidents and approved by respected technical personnel. This will improve the consistency of analysis of repeat failures and reduce the likelihood that others will argue with you after you have decided that a particular failure was a repeat failure.

Check: You have decided that this failure rate is too frequent for the intended purpose of this equipment and that management should do something to make sure that the failure rate is reduced.

Ideas:

- You should continue to analyze the causes to find the Root Causes including corrective actions that have already been developed but have not been implemented (*corrective action not yet implemented*) or corrective actions that need improvement (*corrective action NI*).

Check: You have decided that the problem was caused by failure to provide effective, timely corrective actions for known deficiencies (recurring failures).

Ideas:

- First, you should consider implementing effective, timely corrective actions for the problem that was not corrected that caused you to select this Root Cause.

- Second, you need to consider ways to improve your corrective action system so that effective, timely corrective actions are implemented for identified problems.

- The types of corrective actions needed depend on the reasons for effective, timely corrective actions not being implemented. Therefore, you should consider continuing your investigation to identify correctable causes of the corrective action failures.

Ideas for Generic Problems:

- If you find that failure to implement effective, timely corrective actions is a generic problem, then you should consider continuing your investigation to identify all the problems that are causing the corrective action system to fail and then implement effective corrective actions to improve the system.

corrective action NI:

Check: You have decided that the corrective action recommended in the past needs to be improved. (This may include a lack of corrective action for past incidents.)

Ideas:

- Recommend effective corrective actions! Before you can do this you need to understand the Root Causes of the problem. Therefore, you should continue to analyze the problem's Root Causes.

- Statistical Process Control (SPC) may be helpful in analyzing the causes of repeat failures and in developing corrective actions.

- If you cannot find the problem's Root Causes, then you should consider conducting a Safeguards Analysis (Chapter 10 of the *TapRooT® Book*, 2008) to identify potential Safeguards that you could add to reduce the likelihood of this incident recurring.

- Or you may consider redesigning the equipment to eliminate the process or   equipment that is causing the repeat failures.

- Also, you should keep a list of repeat failures that were attributed to the corrective actions needing improvement. This will improve the consistency of analysis of repeat failures.

- Also, you should consider ways to improve your corrective action system so that effective, timely corrective actions are implemented for identified problems. The types of corrective actions needed depend on the reasons the corrective action needs improvement.
    a. If no corrective action was recommended for a known problem, consider revising your problem reporting and Root cause analysis procedures to include guidance on developing corrective actions for problems.
    b. Also, consider discussing the need for effective corrective actions and how the failure to develop corrective actions caused this problem with management and others involved.
    c. If the corrective action addressed only the symptoms of a problem and failed to address the previous deficiency's Root Causes, consider improving your Root cause analysis system. This may require implementing a state-of-the-art Root cause analysis system (TapRooT®) or improving the use of the system. Review the following to identify potential improvements:
        -   your procedures for Root cause analysis;
        -   the initial training you provide;
        -   specialized training for facilitators & human performance investigators;
        -   continuing training to improve skills;
        -   your review of incident reports and corrective actions; and
        -   the field practices for performing Root cause analysis.
    d. Also, review the "SMARTER" concept provided in Chapter 3 of the *TapRooT® Book*, (2008) for ideas on how to improve corrective actions and make them more effective.
    e. If an effective corrective action was initially proposed, but the corrective action that was implemented was not according to the initial corrective action recommended, find out why the changes

were made and implement corrective action to strengthen the corrective action process.

- Once you have identified corrective actions to improve your corrective action process, you should communicate these improvements to all involved.

Ideas for Generic Problems:

- If you find that ineffective corrective actions are a generic problem, consider conducting an audit of your Root cause analysis and corrective action system. An independent audit would probably be a wise choice for this type of problem so that you could get information about how you compare to others in your industry or other industries.

References:

- For more information about System Improvements' independent audits of Root cause analysis and corrective action systems, call (865) 539-2139.
- For more information about SPC, read *Understanding Statistical Process Control,* (1992) by Donald J. Wheeler and David S. Chambers, and published by SPC Press, Knoxville, TN.

corrective action not yet implemented:

Check: You have decided that the corrective action for a problem that was previously identified was not implemented soon enough.

Ideas:

- First, fix the specific cause of the repeat failure.
  a. Consider recommending action to expedite the implementation of the already existing corrective action.
  b. Consider recommending interim compensatory action that can be implemented immediately as a stop-gap measure (even though it may not be as effective as the more extensive corrective action). The goal of the interim compensatory action is to somewhat reduce the likelihood of the incident recurring or to mitigate the consequences of the incident if it does recur while you implement the longer term corrective action.
  c. If you cannot develop appropriate interim corrective action and if the consequences of another failure of this type are unacceptable, consider stopping production or shutting down the facility until the problem can be corrected.

Ideas for Generic Problems:

- You need to consider ways to improve your corrective action system so that effective corrective actions are implemented in a timely manner. The types of corrective actions needed depend on the reasons the corrective action needs improvement.

- If the corrective action for a known deficiency is not implemented because management did not have the needed resources, consider recommending that in future budget and resource evaluations, a portion of the budget or manpower allocation be set aside for rapid response to implementing corrective actions.

- If the corrective action was not implemented because of problems in project design, abnormal length of the corrective action to implementation cycle, etc., then you should consider recommending a review of these processes with an eye toward a process redesign.

- If the failure to track the implementation of corrective actions leads to unacceptable delays in the implementation of corrective actions, you should consider recommending an accurate and effective corrective action tracking system be implemented.

- If a tracking system was in place but management puts no emphasis on implementing corrective actions, you should consider a management briefing to explain how the lack of emphasis impacted this incident and could impact future incidents.

- If you don't know the causes of the failure to implement corrective actions, consider conducting an audit of your corrective action system.
    a. An independent audit would probably be a wise choice for this type of problem so that you could get information about how you compare to others in your industry, or other industries.
    b. For more information about System Improvements' independent audits of Root cause analysis and corrective action systems, call (865) 539-2139.

- Once you have identified ways to improve your corrective action process, you should communicate these improvements to all involved.

trending NI:

Check: You have decided that the trends from previous incidents or audits/ observations should have been used to identify the problem related to this Causal Factor/issue and, that by using these trends to discover the problem, effective corrective action should have been developed and implemented that would have prevented this incident.

Ideas:

- You should consider recommending improvements to the trending program to correct the problem(s) that allowed the trend to be missed.

Ideas for Generic Problems:

- If failure to detect problems using trends is a generic problem, consider the following improvements for your trending program:
  a. Start collecting your Root cause analysis data in a database so that trending incidents, accidents, and audits/observations is possible using software.
  b. Choose a database and software that allows trending on the Root Cause level as well as other levels in the Root Cause Tree®.
  c. Divide your data into like work types so that trends aren't masked by averaging.
  d. If your data is unreliable, consider improvements in your data analysis and collection system from the *TapRooT® Book,* (2008), Chapter 5, "Collecting Good Data" section.
  e. Use Pareto Charts to identify areas where your improvement efforts will yield the largest payback for the effort invested.
  f. Use Process Behavior Charts to detect trends in data over time.
  g. Use special Process Behavior Charts to detect trends in infrequently occurring data. Interval Process behavior Charts should be used to detect improvements and Rate Process Behavior Charts should be used to spot problems.

References:

- *TapRooT® Book,* (2008) by Mark Paradies and Linda Unger, published by System Improvements, Knoxville, TN. Call (865) 539-2139, see www.taproot.com, or e-mail info@taproot.com.

  For more information about SPC, read:

- *Building Continual Improvement,* (1999) by Donald J. Wheeler and Sheila R. Poling, published by SPC Press, Knoxville, TN.

- *Understanding Statistical Process Control,* (1992) by Donald J. Wheeler and David S. Chambers, and published by SPC Press, Knoxville, TN.

- For training on improved trending, attend the 2-Day TapRooT® Advanced Trending Techniques Course. For information see www.taproot.com, or call (865) 539-2139, or e-mail info@taproot.com.

LEVEL 2:
Human Performance Troubleshooting Guide
(15 Questions)

15 Questions

For each of the 15 Questions, you have decided that this problem was caused by a Human Performance Difficulty, but you have not progressed down the Root Cause Tree® to the Root Cause level.

Ideas:

- Effective corrective action based on Root cause analysis is not possible unless you progress further down the Root Cause Tree®.

- If you cannot progress further down the tree, then consider performing a Safeguards Analysis (Chapter 10 of the *TapRooT® Book*, 2008) to identify potential Safeguards that you could add to reduce the likelihood of this incident recurring.

- If you are investigating an equipment problem, consider using Equifactor® to troubleshoot the cause of the problem.

LEVELS 3 – 5: Procedures

PROCEDURES

Check: You have decided that the problem was related to written procedure use, lack of a written procedure, or misuse of a written procedure.

Ideas:

- You should continue to analyze the cause of this problem to find the Root Cause of the procedure problem. You can then correct the Root Causes.

- If you can't identify the Root Causes, then perform a Safeguards Analysis (Chapter 10 of the *TapRooT® Book*, 2008) to identify potential Safeguards that you could add to reduce the likelihood of this problem recurring.

- Don't try to use written procedures (checklists) to fix every problem. For example, not all problems or poorly human factored designs can be expected to be overcome by providing detailed procedures to "work-around" poorly human factored designs. Therefore, if you find that a procedure is a substitute for a better designed human-machine interface, consider improving the ergonomics or human factors design of the equipment rather than trying to improve the procedure.

- Also, you may want to consider recommending training people if reasonable amounts of additional training would help people successfully complete the work when using written procedures.

- Also, you should consider recommending training about the procedure changes that you make for the people who use the procedures.

References:

- For more information about the theory behind procedure usage and writing effective procedures, we recommend attending the 5-Day TapRooT® Advanced Root Cause Analysis Team Leader Training. For more information call (865) 539-2139, or see www.taproot.com/courses.php.

- Also, you may read *Procedure Writing Principles and Practices,* (1998) by Douglas Wieringa, Christopher Moore, and Valerie Barnes, and published by Battelle Press, Columbus, Ohio.

- Code of Federal Regulations (Pharmaceuticals) 21CFR211.100, *Written Procedures*

Not Used / Not Followed

Check: You have decided that properly using a procedure to perform this task would have prevented or significantly reduced the consequences of this incident.

Ideas:

- You should continue to analyze the cause of this problem to find the Root Cause of the procedure problem. You can then correct the Root Causes.

- If you can't identify the Root Causes, then perform a Safeguards Analysis (Chapter 10 of the *TapRooT® Book,* 2008) to identify potential Safeguards that you could add to reduce the likelihood of this problem recurring.

- Don't try to use written procedures (checklists) to fix every problem. For example, not all problems or poorly human factored designs can be expected to be overcome by providing detailed procedures to "work-around" poorly human factored designs. Therefore, if you find that a procedure is a substitute for a better designed human-machine interface, consider improving the ergonomics or human factors design of the equipment rather than trying to improve the procedure.

- Also, you may want to consider recommending training people if reasonable amounts of additional training would help people successfully complete the work when using procedures.

- Also, you should consider recommending training about the procedure changes that you make for the people who use the procedures.

- If a procedure was available and was required to be used but was not used or was consciously not followed or deviated from, then the corrective actions will be found under the Management System - SPAC Not Used portion of the Root Cause Tree®.

Ideas for Generic Problems:

- If people not using or not following procedures is a generic problem, you should consider implementing a program to correct the problem.

- One idea to start the development of a program would be to survey employees (either verbally or in writing) about procedure usage and procedure problems to identify the causes for the problems.

- Also, you would probably perform field audits or reviews to identify Root Causes of procedure usage problems.

- Then you would develop a procedure usage improvement program based on your observations, Root cause analysis, and discussions with managers and employees. You would then roll out the program with appropriate training for those affected.

- You should also consider instituting continuing procedure usage audits to see if your improvements worked and to identify any new problems that might occur.

References:

- *Achieving 100% Compliance of Policies and Procedures,* (2000) by Stephen Page, published by Process Improvement Publishers.

- *Procedure Writing Principles and Practices,* (1998) by Douglas Wieringa, Christopher Moore, and Valerie Barnes, published by Battelle Press, Columbus, Ohio.

- For more information about the theory behind procedure usage and writing effective procedures, we recommend attending the 5-Day TapRooT® Advanced Root Cause Analysis Team Leader Training. For more information call (865) 539-2139, or see www.taproot.com/courses. php. For more help developing a procedure usage improvement program contact System Improvements by calling (865) 539-2139.

no procedure:

Check: Your analysis has shown that there was no procedure to perform this work, and you have decided that using a good procedure would improve performance of this task.

Ideas:

- You should consider recommending the development of a procedure to perform this task because procedures can help people perform more reliably. However, not all tasks are improved by procedures.
    a. Before recommending the development of a procedure, you must decide if using a procedure would improve performance. Some

tasks that should probably have procedures include those that could result in unacceptable consequences if not performed exactly right (for example, failure to set the flaps during takeoff in a commercial airliner), tasks that require documentation (for example, assembly of nuclear fuel), tasks that require considerable amounts of short term memory (for example, performing a valve line-up of 50 valves), tasks that are performed infrequently (for example, plant start-ups that are performed only about once a year), and tasks that are performed under stress or with frequent interruptions (for example, emergency response procedures for a plant upset).

    b.   Other tasks may not be improved by using a procedure. For example, not all problems or poorly human factored designs can be expected to be overcome by providing detailed procedures to "work-around" poorly human factored designs. Therefore, if you find that a procedure is a substitute for a better designed human-machine interface, consider improving the ergonomics or human factors design of the equipment rather than trying to improve the procedure.

- If you recommend development of a procedure, also consider recommending training for the users of the procedure. This may include training for the current users and training for trainees. Consider including in the training the reason for the procedure, proper usage of the procedure, and any skills required to use the procedure.

Ideas for Generic Problems:

- If you find that a lack of procedures is a generic problem, consider recommending guidance for operations and maintenance as to when they should have a procedure to perform a task.

- Once you have developed guidance for when a procedure should be used, you may consider performing a systematic assessment of the tasks performed to decide which ones need to have procedures developed.

- Once you develop new procedures you would conduct training for the people affected so that they understand the new procedures and the reason for them.

References:

- For more information about the theory behind procedure usage and writing effective procedures, we recommend attending the 5-Day TapRooT® Advanced Root Cause Analysis Team Leader Training. For more information call (865) 539-2139, or see www.taproot.com/courses.php.

- *Procedure Writing Principles and Practices,* (1998) by Douglas Wieringa, Christopher Moore, and Valerie Barnes, published by Battelle Press, Columbus, Ohio.

- *7 Steps to Better Written Policies and Procedures,* (2001) by Stephen Page, published by Process Improvement Publishing.

procedure not available or inconvenient for use:

Check: You have decided that the procedure was not used because it was not readily available or it could not be conveniently used.

Ideas:

- You should consider recommending ways to make the procedure available and convenient at the worksite. Don't be limited by the methods that have been used in the past! Just because the current system keeps all the procedures in the Administration Building doesn't mean that they can't be made available in the field. Ideas to consider include:
  a. posting a durable copy of the procedure at the workstation,
  b. providing field copies of the procedures,
  c. providing disposable copies of the procedure, or
  d. providing the procedure user with some electronic or audible form of the procedure.

- Once you have found how to make the procedure available to those who need to use it, consider recommending training for the users to explain what you've done and why it is important for them to use the procedure.

Ideas for Generic Problems:

- If you find that the availability of procedures is a generic problem, consider recommending a systematic change the makes all procedures more available to the people who need to use them.

- Don't forget to train people about the change so that they understand the way you are making procedures more available.

procedure difficult to use:

Check: You have decided that the procedure was not used because it was difficult to use.

Ideas:

- You should consider recommending ways to make the procedure easier to use. Of course, making each procedure easier to use depends on the specific procedure, but here are some ideas to consider:
  a. lower the required reading level.
  b. simplify the steps.
  c. rewrite the procedure so that it can be performed more efficiently.
  d. flow charting a procedure that contains complex decisions.
  e. change the procedure's level of detail to make it appropriate for the user's skill level.

    One way to start this process is to ask the procedure users what they would like to see in the procedure. This may not work if the procedure users can't see beyond the current procedures that they are accustomed to NOT using.

- If you think that additional training could have raised the procedure user's skill level so that the procedure would have been usable, you should also consider recommending training for the personnel who perform the work.

- If you think that additional preparation for the work could have raised the procedure user's knowledge level so that the procedure would have been usable, consider recommending additional preparation for the work. For example, a pre-job brief or a walk-thru by the supervisor that shows the worker how to use the procedure might make the procedure easier to use.

- As part of your recommendation, you should consider having users field test the revised procedure to ensure that it is easier to use.

- Once you have improved the procedure's usability, recommend training for the procedure users to let them know that you have changed the procedure, how you have changed it, and how they should use it.

- If you can't find a way to make the procedure more usable, you may want to consider re-engineering the process to change the work so that the work is easier to perform (and the procedure easier to use). This may require changing the human-machine interface or changing the process lay out. As with all major changes, the cost and benefit of radical redesign needs to be considered. But don't let the standard response of "We've always done it this way" stop you from considering innovative ways to change the work or the procedure to make the procedure or the work less difficult.

- Also, consider performing a Safeguards Analysis if a difficult to use procedure is the only barrier between success and a serious accident. For more information about Safeguards Analysis, see Chapter 10 of the *TapRooT® Book,* (2008).

Procedures (Not Used/Not Followed)

Ideas for Generic Problems:

- If you find that the usability of procedures is a generic problem, consider recommending guidance and training for procedure writers to improve the usability of written procedures.

- Also, consider recommending a complete procedure improvement program to improve the usability of all your procedures before additional incidents occur.

References:

- To learn more about the proper way to write procedures to make them more usable, we recommend attending the 5-Day TapRooT® Advanced Root Cause Analysis Team Leader Training. For more information call (865) 539-2139, or see www.taproot.com/courses.php.

- *Procedure Writing Principles and Practices,* (1998) by Douglas Wieringa, Christopher Moore, and Valerie Barnes, published by Battelle Press, Columbus, Ohio.

- To get help developing a procedure improvement program call System Improvements at (865) 539-2139.

procedure use not required but should be:

Check: You have found that a procedure did exist for this task but wasn't used because it was not required to be used and you decided that this procedure should be required to be used.

Ideas:

- You should consider recommending that the procedure be required for performance of this task.

- Requiring the use of this procedure may not be enough to actually get the people who perform the task to actually use the procedure. Therefore, you should consider ideas to increase the likelihood that the procedure will be used. How? The following are a few ideas:
  a. Require a signature at the end of the procedure.
  b. Make the procedure a checklist and require the completed checklist to be attached to the completed work order.
  c. Have management and supervision audit the usage of the procedure in the field.
  d. Post the procedure at the worksite.
  e. Integrate the procedure into the work. (Examples: Put the space for calculations in the procedure. Put key tables or charts in the procedure. Include valve line-up checklists in the procedure. Put

the procedure on a distributed control system and integrate the steps with action buttons to make the actions happen.)

    f.   Get user suggestions on increasing the usability of the procedure.

- Also, if you now require people to use a procedure that previously had been optional, you need to tell the users about the change!

- Also, you should always train the people performing the work why using the procedure is important to successful performance. Hands-on demonstrations of the impact are especially effective in convincing people that change is needed.

Ideas for Generic Problems:

- If you find that failure to require the use of procedures is a generic problem, then you should consider recommending the development of a policy or standard on procedure usage. See the Management System – Standards, Policies, or Administrative Controls NI section for more suggested corrective actions to solve this type of generic problem.

- If the procedure was consciously not followed because a deviation from the procedure was allowed without adequate review, then requiring procedure usage will not be enough (because the procedure might be modified without adequate review, and the modification might cause problems). Again, this might point to a generic problem with the management control of procedures. If you find that failure to require sufficient review of procedure modifications is a generic problem, then you should consider recommending the development of a policy or standard on procedure modification. See the Management Systems – Standards, Policies, or Administrative Controls NI section for more suggested corrective actions to solve this type of generic problem.

References:

- *Achieving 100% Compliance of Policies and Procedures,* (2000) by Stephen Page, published by Process Improvement Publishing.

Wrong

Check: You decided that the procedure that was used was wrong.

Ideas:

- You should continue to analyze the cause of this problem to find out how and why the procedure was wrong. You can then correct the Root Causes and rewrite the procedure so that it is right.

- Remember to consider recommending training for the procedure users about any corrections to the procedure.

Ideas for Generic Problems:

- If you find that procedures being wrong is a generic problem, you should consider ways to improve the procedure production process to reduce the likelihood of publishing procedures that are wrong.

- One idea to help you develop an improved procedure production process would be to benchmark your practices against other companies known for their excellent performance. Then take the ideas you discover and modify your procedure writing and review process to include the good practices that you learn. Finally, train the people who write procedures on these new processes.

References:

- For more information about developing good procedures, we recommend attending the 5-Day TapRooT® Advanced Root Cause Analysis Team Leader Training. For more information call (865) 539-2139, or see www.taproot.com/courses.php.

- *Procedure Writing Principles and Practices,* (1998) by Douglas Wieringa, Christopher Moore, and Valerie Barnes, published by Battelle Press, Columbus, Ohio.

typo:

Check: You have decided that a typographical error was responsible for the incident.

Ideas:

- Consider recommending correcting the typographical error.

- Once you have corrected the procedure, notify the procedure users that the typo has been corrected.

- This may be a good time to reinforce the actions to be taken if the procedure users find mistakes (like typos) in a procedure so that the mistakes can be corrected before an incident occurs.

Ideas for Generic Problems:

- If you find that typographical errors and other mistakes are a generic procedure problem, then you need to recommend changes to the procedure writing and review process to improve procedure quality.

- If you find that typographical errors and other mistakes are a generic procedure problem and you correct the procedure system, then you need to consider recommending a general procedure improvement program to remove the existing typographical errors and other mistakes from the procedures.

- Consider simultaneously implementing other improvements to the procedures.

References:

- To learn methods for improving your procedures, attend the 5-Day TapRooT® Advanced Root Cause Analysis Team Leader Training. For more information call (865) 539-2139, or see www.taproot.com/courses.php.

- *Procedure Writing Principles and Practices,* (1998) by Douglas Wieringa, Christopher Moore, and Valerie Barnes, published by Battelle Press, Columbus, Ohio.

sequence wrong:

Check: You have found that the problem occurred because the sequence of the procedure steps was wrong.

Ideas:

- Consider recommending the procedure be modified so that the sequence is correct.

- Consider not only making the sequence technically accurate but also optimize the procedure so that it improves the efficiency of the work. Make sure you consider the physical layout of the equipment and any human limitations.

- Once you have corrected the procedure, notify the procedure users that the sequence has been corrected.

- This may be a good time to reinforce the actions to be taken if the procedure users find mistakes (like sequence problems) in a procedure so that the mistakes can be corrected before an incident occurs.

Ideas for Generic Problems:

- If you find that sequence problems and other mistakes are a generic procedure problem, recommend changes to the procedure writing and review process to improve the quality of your procedures.

- If you find that sequence problems and other mistakes are a generic procedure problem and if you correct the procedure system, then consider recommending a general procedure improvement program to remove the existing sequence problems and other mistakes from the procedures.

- Consider other improvements to the procedures be implemented at the same time.

References:

- To learn methods for improving your procedures, attend the 5-Day TapRooT® Advanced Root Cause Analysis Team Leader Training. For more information call (865) 539-2139, or see www.taproot.com/courses.php.

- *Procedure Writing Principles and Practices,* (1998) by Douglas Wieringa, Christopher Moore, and Valerie Barnes, published by Battelle Press, Columbus, Ohio.

facts wrong:

Check: You have found that the incident occurred because the steps in the procedure were factually incorrect.

Ideas:

- You should consider recommending the procedure be corrected with the proper factual information.

- Once you have corrected the factual content of the procedure, notify the procedure users of the changes.

- Also, this may be a good time to reinforce the actions to be taken if the procedure users find factual inaccuracies in a procedure so that the mistakes can be corrected before an incident occurs.

Ideas for Generic Problems:

- If you find that inaccurate factual content in the procedures is a generic problem, recommend changes to the procedure writing and review process.

- If you find that inaccurate factual content is a generic procedure problem and if you correct the procedure system, then you need to consider recommending a general procedure improvement program to improve the factual content of the procedures.

- You may want to consider simultaneously implementing other improvements to the procedures.

References:

- To learn methods for improving your procedures, attend the 5-Day TapRooT® Advanced Root Cause Analysis Team Leader Training. For more information call (865) 539-2139, or see www.taproot.com/courses.php.

- *Procedure Writing Principles and Practices,* (1998) by Douglas Wieringa, Christopher Moore, and Valerie Barnes, published by Battelle Press, Columbus, Ohio.

situation not covered:

Check: You have decided that the procedure failed to address all situations that reasonably should have been expected to occur during completion of the procedure.

Ideas:

• You should consider recommending an addition to the procedure that covers the situation that caused the incident.

• You should also consider recommending training for the procedure users on the situation that caused the problem so that they understand the situation and how the procedure should be used in that situation.

• Once you have corrected the scope of the procedure so that it covers all the situations that should reasonably be included, notify the procedure users.

• Also, this may be a good time to reinforce the actions to be taken if the procedure users find other procedures with omissions so that the omissions can be corrected before an incident occurs.

Ideas for Generic Problems:

• If you find that the scope of the procedures not covering situations adequately is a generic problem, then you need to recommend changes to the procedure writing and review process.

• Also, consider recommending a general procedure improvement program to improve the scope of the procedures.

• You may want to consider implementing other improvements to the procedures at the same time.

References:

• To learn methods for improving your procedures, attend the 5-Day TapRooT® Advanced Root Cause Analysis Team Leader Training. For more information call (865) 539-2139, or see www.taproot.com/courses.php.

• *Procedure Writing Principles and Practices,* (1998) by Douglas Wieringa, Christopher Moore, and Valerie Barnes, published by Battelle Press, Columbus, Ohio.

wrong revision used:

Check: You have found that the wrong revision of a procedure was used and that if the correct revision would have been used, the problem would not have occurred or would have been less severe.

Ideas:

- You should consider recommending improvements to reduce the likelihood that the wrong revision of a procedure will be used. This can include:
  a. eliminate old copies of the procedure,
  b. keep only the current revision of the procedure in the field, and
  c. improve the process for entering temporary procedure changes.

- Some may suggest implementing an electronic procedure system so that only the most recent procedure revision with the appropriate temporary procedure changes is available to be printed out. Proceed with caution! The electronic system must meet the needs of the user. The electronic system must be at least as easy to use, if not more easy to use, than the old paper based system. Also, make sure that procedure users don't keep copies of old procedures or you may be introducing another way for the wrong revision of the procedure to get to the field. Also, consider what might happen if a power or computer outage reduced access to the procedures. And finally, consider the pace of operations and the usage "load" to see if your automation can handle the usage that it will receive in an outage or turnaround (high usage operations).

- Once the proper revisions of the procedure are available, make sure that the procedure users understand which revision is to be used, how they are to obtain the proper revision, and what they can do to make sure that the proper revision of a procedure is used.

Ideas for Generic Problems:

- If you find that using the wrong revision of the procedure is a generic problem, then you should consider revising the procedure distribution system so that the wrong revisions of procedures are not available in the field.

- Make sure that when you fix this generic problem that you inform the procedure users what you have done to improve the availability of the proper revision of procedures and what they are supposed to do to make the system work.

References:

- To learn methods for improving your procedures, attend the 5-Day TapRooT® Advanced Root Cause Analysis Team Leader Training. For more information call (865) 539-2139, or see www.taproot.com/courses.php.

- *Procedure Writing Principles and Practices,* (1998) by Douglas Wieringa, Christopher Moore, and Valerie Barnes, published by Battelle Press, Columbus, Ohio.

Procedures (Wrong)

- *7 Steps to Better Written Policies and Procedures,* (2001) by Steve Page, published by Process Improvement Publishing.

second checker needed:

Check: You have decided that a second checker should have been used as part of this task and that one should have been included in the procedure.

Ideas:

- Consider recommending the use of a second checker as a part of the procedure.

- Using a second checker is not appropriate for all work. A second person to watch work is expensive and many would argue that it decreases the perceived responsibility of the worker performing the task. Therefore, you may be reluctant to recommend the use of a second checker without real and convincing evidence that the work is so dangerous or so important that absolute mistake free operation is required.

- Even in the case where you decide that the work is absolutely critical, you should be aware that a second checker is a weak Safeguard to additional mistakes. It will take great effort on the part of the second checker not to be lulled into a sense of complacency by tasks that are repeatedly performed correctly and infrequently performed incorrectly. This is an innate part of human nature. The second checker may even "see" what he wants to see (correct performance) when in reality, a mistake was made. Therefore, you may want to perform a Safeguards Analysis to see if any other, potentially more effective Safeguards could be used rather than requiring a second checker. For more information on Safeguards Analysis, see Chapter 10 of the *TapRooT® Book,* (2008).

- If you find that a second checker is required, then you must thoroughly convince those performing the work of the essential requirement to have a second checker.

- You will also need to consider audits to check the second checker's performance. (Have an occasional third checker!)

- You may also consider running drills (intentional false alarms) to increase the stimuli (signals or mistakes) that the second checker is looking for. Make sure that these drills don't cause unintended incidents.

Ideas for Generic Problems:

- Because you probably won't recommend extensive use of second checkers, it is unlikely that the lack of a second checker will be a generic problem.

- If you find that the lack of a second checker is a generic problem, you should consider changing the process to reduce the risk or consider recommending implementation of some type of automated monitoring to improve performance (rather than having dozens or hundreds of second checkers).

Followed Incorrectly

Check: You have decided that the procedure was used and was technically correct but, for some reason, the person did not follow it correctly. Also, you believe that following the procedure correctly would have prevented or significantly mitigated the problem.

Ideas:

- You should continue to analyze the reason that the procedure was followed incorrectly to find the Root Cause or causes. You can then correct the Root Cause(s).

- If you can't find a Root Cause under the followed incorrectly section of the Root Cause Tree®, then you should consider Root Causes under the Human Engineering and Training sections of the tree.

- If you can't identify the Root Causes in those sections of the tree, then perform a Safeguards Analysis (Chapter 10 of the *TapRooT® Book,* 2008) to identify potential Safeguards that you could add to reduce the likelihood of this problem recurring even if the procedure is followed incorrectly.

References:

- For more information about the theory behind procedure usage and writing effective procedures that can be followed correctly, we recommend attending the 5-Day TapRooT® Advanced Root Cause Analysis Team Leader Training. For more information call (865) 539-2139, or see www.taproot.com/courses.php.

- *Procedure Writing Principles and Practices,* (1998) by Douglas Wieringa, Christopher Moore, and Valerie Barnes, published by Battelle Press, Columbus, Ohio.

format confusing:

Check: You have decided that the procedure was followed incorrectly because the procedure format kept the reader from easily, rapidly, and precisely understanding the procedure's intent.

Ideas:

- You should become familiar with the procedure formats and writing techniques that make procedures easy to read.

- Also, you should be able to evaluate a procedure for its grade level, complexity, and specificity.

- Then consider recommending how to improve the procedure so that the format makes the procedure easy to use.

- Once you have revised the procedure, test the procedure in the field to make sure that a variety of the procedure users accurately and consistently use the procedure.

Ideas for Generic Problems:

- If you find that confusing procedure formats are a generic problem, you should consider recommending the development of format guidance and training for procedure writers so that the procedures they develop are consistently easy to use.

- Consider recommending a formal procedure review to check each new procedure against the procedure format guidance.

- Consider recommending a field review to assess the usability of procedures.

- If you find that confusing procedure formats are a generic problem, once your procedure system has been improved and appropriate guidance is in place, then you should consider a procedure improvement program to improve the already existing confusing procedures.

- If you correct confusing procedures, inform the procedure users of the changes and why the changes were made. They also should understand why the format was chosen and how it will improve their performance.

- This might be a good time to reinforce the actions to be taken if the procedure users identify a procedure that they think is confusing or that doesn't meet the approved procedure format.

References:

- To learn more about improving the format of procedures, attend the 5-Day TapRooT® Advanced Root Cause Analysis Team Leader Training. For more information call (865) 539-2139, or see www. taproot.com/courses.php.

- *Procedure Writing Principles and Practices,* (1998) by Douglas Wieringa, Christopher Moore, and Valerie Barnes, published by Battelle Press, Columbus, Ohio.

> 1 action per step:

Check: You have decided that the problem occurred because a procedural step had more than one action (rather than in crisp, single action statements).

Ideas:

- You should consider recommending re-writing the procedure with a single action in each step.

- If the procedure user could lose his place in the procedure, consider recommending adding a space for a check mark at the end of each step.

Ideas for Generic Problems:

- If you find that procedures having more than one action per step are a generic problem, consider recommending guidance for procedure writers.

- Also, consider training the procedure writers about this guidance.

- Also, during the review of a new procedure, consider adding a specific check to make sure that there is only one action per step.

- Once you have these generic corrective actions in place, consider recommending a general procedure improvement program to remove multiple actions per step from the rest of the facility's procedures.

- Once the general procedure improvement program is implemented, make sure that you explain to the procedure users why the changes are being made and how the changes are intended to improve their performance.

- Also, this may be a good time to reinforce the actions to be taken if the procedure users find problems (like procedures with more than one action per step) in a procedure so that the problems can be corrected before an incident occurs.

References:

- To learn more about improving procedures, attend the 5-Day TapRooT® Advanced Root Cause Analysis Team Leader Training. For more information call (865) 539-2139, or see www.taproot.com/courses.php.

- *Procedure Writing Principles and Practices,* (1998) by Douglas Wieringa, Christopher Moore, and Valerie Barnes, published by Battelle Press, Columbus, Ohio.

Procedures (Followed Incorrectly)

excess references:

Check: You have decided that one procedure referring to additional procedures caused the user to become confused, lose his/her place, or omit steps in one of the multiple procedures.

Ideas:

- You should consider recommending a revision of the procedure to include all the information needed by the procedure user (reducing the number of references).

- If this isn't possible, you should consider other aids that could help consolidate the information needed by the procedure user. This could include some type of computerized artificial intelligence (AI) program, a database of information, or an overall flowchart of how the work is performed and how the procedures are related.

Ideas for Generic Problems:

- If excessive references are a generic problem, your facility probably has a complex, interrelated procedure system. Simplifying the complex interrelating procedures should improve the procedure user's performance. However, this will not be an easy problem to solve. You could provide an AI program, or you may decide that simplifying the process (through re-engineering) is a better solution.

multiple unit references:

Check: You have decided that the procedure user was confused by the procedure containing references to multiple plants or units.

Ideas:

- You should consider recommending the development of separate procedures for each plant or unit.

- Once separate procedures have been developed, make sure that you explain to the procedure users why the changes are being made and how the changes are intended to improve their performance.

- Also, this may be a good time to reinforce the actions to be taken if the procedure users find problems (like multiple unit references) in a procedure so that the problems can be corrected before an incident occurs.

Ideas for Generic Problems:

- If multiple unit references causing procedures to be confusing is a generic problem, you need to consider recommending the development

Procedures (Followed Incorrectly)

of separate procedures for each plant or unit for all the procedures that are used by both plants or units.

limits NI:

Check: You have decided that the problem occurred because the limits or permissible operating ranges were not expressed in absolute numbers but instead expressed in a "+ or -" format. (For example, expressing the limits as "1.39 ± 0.69" is much more likely to cause errors than using "0.70 to 2.08".)

Ideas:

- You should consider recommending that the procedure be rewritten using absolute numbers to express ranges rather than a ± number. For example, if the procedure read:

    18. Adjust the potentiometer until the output meter reads 65 volts (±14%).

Then you should recommend that it be changed to read:

    18. Adjust the potentiometer until the output meter reads about 65 volts (meter reading between 55.9 and 74.1 volts).

- People are notorious for making simple math errors. Changing the way you express these limits will relieve the procedure user of having to perform mental math to find the correct limits.

Ideas for Generic Problems:

- If you find that procedures having ranges expressed in a "±" format is a generic problem, consider recommending guidance for procedure writers.

- Also, consider training the procedure writers about this guidance.

- Also, during the review of a new procedure, consider adding a specific check to make sure that ranges are not expressed in a "±" format.

- Once you have these generic corrective actions in place, consider recommending a general procedure improvement program to remove ranges that are expressed in a "±" format.

- Once the general procedure improvement program is implemented, make sure that you explain to the procedure users why the changes are being made and how the changes are intended to improve their performance.

- Also, this may be a good time to reinforce the actions to be taken if the procedure users find problems (like procedures with "±" numbers) in a procedure so that the problems can be corrected before an incident occurs.

Procedures (Followed Incorrectly)

References:

- To learn more about improving procedures, attend the 5-Day TapRooT® Advanced Root Cause Analysis Team Leader Training. For more information call (865) 539-2139, or see www.taproot.com/courses.php.

- *Procedure Writing Principles and Practices*, (1998) by Douglas Wieringa, Christopher Moore, and Valerie Barnes, published by Battelle Press, Columbus, Ohio.

details NI:

Check: You have decided that the problem was caused by a procedure being written at an inappropriate level of detail given the training and experience required for personnel performing the work.

Ideas:

- Consider recommending that the procedure be rewritten at the appropriate level of detail.

- Often procedures are written at the wrong level of detail. (For example, "replace the pump" is one action that may require many implicit steps, including tagging out the pump and disconnecting fluid lines and electrical power.) Why? Because the procedure writer wrote the procedure for his own experience level rather than the experience level of the user. Or because the previous procedure was written at that level of detail. Or because the procedure writer didn't have time to research all of the details. The level of detail of a procedure should be based on:
  - The purpose of the procedure.
  - The range of experience and training of the people performing the work.
  - The complexity or difficulty of the task.
  - How often the task is performed.
  - How much risk is involved in the work.
  - Requirements for documentation of the work.

- Procedures can also have too much detail. Too much information included in action steps can cause procedures users to stop using the procedure or to skim over important information. If this is the problem, consider revising the procedure to provide the right level of detail. You may also consider providing a dual column format with a summary of the actions in one column and the detailed steps in another.

- Once you have developed a procedure that you believe is at the appropriate level of detail, you should have the procedure users review it. To make the review more meaningful, the reviewers should understand the reason for the level of detail that you have chosen.

Ideas for Generic Problems:

- If you find that the level of detail in procedures is a generic problem, consider recommending additional guidance and training for procedure writers so that they start to consider the appropriate level of detail when they are writing procedures.

- Consider making an evaluation of the level of detail of the procedure a standard part of the procedure review process.

- Once you have trained the procedure writers and modified the review process, consider recommending a procedure upgrade program to rewrite the current procedures at the appropriate level of detail.

- Once the procedure upgrade program is implemented, make sure that you explain to the procedure users why the changes are being made and how the changes are intended to improve their performance.

- Also, this may be a good time to reinforce the actions to be taken if the procedure users find problems (like inadequate details) in a procedure so that the problems can be corrected before an incident occurs.

References:

- If you have trouble determining the appropriate level of detail for the procedure, you should consider learning more about procedure writing. We recommend attending the 5-Day TapRooT® Advanced Root Cause Analysis Team Leader Training. For more information call (865) 539-2139, or see www.taproot.com/courses.php.

- *Procedure Writing Principles and Practices,* (1998) by Douglas Wieringa, Christopher Moore, and Valerie Barnes, published by Battelle Press, Columbus, Ohio.

data/computations wrong or incomplete:

Check: You have decided that the problem was caused by a mistake in recording or transferring data or because of incorrect calculations.

Ideas:

- Consider recommending ways to make the calculation or data collection more accurate, complete, and precise.

- Consider recommending a second check for any critical calculations. (People are notoriously bad at even the simplest addition and subtraction. If you doubt this, how many times have you made mistakes in balancing your checkbook?)

- Ideas for improving the accuracy, completeness, and precision of calculations / data collection include:
  a. Providing space to write down the numbers in a formatted calculation. For example:

     NPSH = 2.3*[(P:_____)-(VP:_____)] = _____ ft of head
  b. Providing a calculator or spreadsheet to perform the math.
  c. Having all critical calculations independently performed by two individuals and compared by a third individual.
  d. Computerizing the collection, recording, and calculations required on all data.
  e. Bar coding for data collection/input of data.
- If you plan to recommend changes, review your preliminary proposals with the intended users to get their ideas on the improvements and possible better alternatives.

Ideas for Generic Problems:

- If you find that data collection and computations are a generic problem, then you should consider changing the way the work is performed (using the guidance above) and developing guidance for the procedure writers so that they provide adequate room to perform calculations and require independent calculations and comparisons of the independent calculations.

- Once these changes have been made, you can then consider recommending a general procedure improvement program to correct the existing procedures that require data collection and calculations.

- Once the procedure improvement program is implemented, make sure that you explain to the procedure users why the changes are being made and how the changes help their performance.

- This may be a good time to reinforce the actions to be taken if the procedure users find problems (like inadequate room to perform calculations) in a procedure so that the problems can be corrected before an incident occurs.

References:
- To learn more about improving procedures, attend the 5-Day TapRooT® Advanced Root Cause Analysis Team Leader Training. For more information call (865) 539-2139, or see www.taproot.com/courses.php.
- *Procedure Writing Principles and Practices,* (1998) by Douglas Wieringa, Christopher Moore, and Valerie Barnes, published by Battelle Press, Columbus, Ohio.

Procedures (Followed Incorrectly)

Check: You have decided that the problem was related to unclear, confusing, or misleading graphs, illustrations, one-line diagrams, or system drawings in the procedure.

Ideas:

- Consider recommending ways to make the graphics clearer, less confusing, or less misleading.

- Ideas for improving graphics include:
  a. Drawings
     - Only use drawings from a vendor manual if they are clear and reproducible.
     - Avoid photographs. They don't copy well and often have too much detail.
     - Produce drawings with clear, unbroken lines.
     - Avoid shading. It doesn't copy well.
     - KISS (Keep It Simple Stupid). Avoid needless detail.
     - Place labels (callouts) so that they aren't cluttered or confusing.
     - Place numbered callouts so that they are in order either horizontally or vertically (whichever makes the most sense).
  b. Graphs
     - Match the scale on the graph to the scale on the equipment, the scale required by the task, and the accuracy required by the procedure.
     - Use heavier lines for the axis than for the grid.
     - Vary the line thickness every fifth line to make the graph easier to read.
  c. Tables
     - Use vertical lines between columns unless there is plenty of white space.
     - Align column headers exactly with columns.
     - Separate column headers from columns with lines or by using bold type or both.
     - Use groups of five rows with margins between them to let the eye more easily track rows.
  d. Copying
     - Don't reduce things more than 50% or to the point that type will be smaller than 5 point.
     - Assume all procedures will be copied before they are used. If you can't read it after you copy it, don't use it in the procedure.
     - Always start with an original or first generation copy to produce a procedure. Starting with a copy of a copy of a copy is bound to produce poor results.

Ideas for Generic Problems:

- If you find that poor graphics are a generic problem, you should consider recommending a graphics improvement program. This may require the help of a professional graphics firm. Make sure they understand the guidance provided above and test a small batch of revised graphics with the procedure users to make sure that their improvements actually improve performance.

- Also provide guidance for the development of future procedures (or for procedure revisions) so that the graphics produced for future procedures meet the new standards of usability.

- Once the graphics improvement program is implemented, make sure that you explain to the procedure users why the changes are being made and how the changes are intended to improve their performance.

- This may be a good time to reinforce the actions to be taken if the procedure users find problems (like bad graphics) in a procedure so that the problems can be corrected before an incident occurs.

References:

- To learn more about improving procedures, attend the 5-Day TapRooT® Advanced Root Cause Analysis Team Leader Training. For more information call (865) 539-2139, or see www.taproot.com/courses.php.

- *Procedure Writing Principles and Practices,* (1998) by Douglas Wieringa, Christopher Moore, and Valerie Barnes, published by Battelle Press, Columbus, Ohio.

no checkoff:

Check: You have decided that the problem was caused by skipping a procedural step or action because each separate action did not have a checkoff space.

Ideas:

- You should consider recommending that the procedure be rewritten with a checkoff space after each action step. An example is provided below:

    4.   Close the acid tank outlet valve (V-231).   _____
                                    CAUTION
    In the next step, filling the tank to 50 gallons should take no longer than 10 minutes. Filling times longer than 10 minutes indicate a problem. Stop filling the tank while you find the cause of the problem.

5. Add 50 gallons of dissolver solution to the acid tank by:
   a. Open the dissolver isolation valve (V-232) and record the time that you started filling the tank. _____

Ideas for Generic Problems:

- If a lack of checkoff spaces is a generic problem, consider developing guidance for including checkoff spaces in procedures.

- Procedure writers should consider including checkoff spaces in procedures that are complex, have extensive valve line ups, have significant risk if a step is omitted, or need documentation that each step was performed.

- Once guidance for procedure writers is in place, be sure to train the procedure writers on the guidance and consider adding a step to the procedure review process to check for checkoff spaces in procedures that meet the guidance.

- Once the checkoffs are in place, make sure that you explain to the procedure users and their supervisors the reason for the checkoffs, how the checkoff is designed to improve their performance, and the proper way to use the checkoff.

- You should also consider having supervisory observations of procedures being used to make sure that checkoffs are being used correctly.

References:

- To learn more about improving procedures, attend the 5-Day TapRooT® Advanced Root Cause Analysis Team Leader Training. For more information call (865) 539-2139, or see www.taproot.com/courses.php.

- *Procedure Writing Principles and Practices,* (1998) by Douglas Wieringa, Christopher Moore, and Valerie Barnes, published by Battelle Press, Columbus, Ohio.

checkoff misused:

Check: You have decided that the problem was caused by a checkoff being misused.

Ideas:

- You should consider recommending corrective actions to ensure that procedure users properly use checkoff spaces. What type of corrective actions? This depends on the reason that the checkoff was misused.

- If the checkoff was misused because the procedure didn't implement checkoffs well, consider rewriting the procedure. An example of a good checkoff is provided below:

- The checkoff might have been misused because the procedure user didn't understand the reason for the checkoffs, how the checkoff is designed to improve their performance, and the proper way to use the checkoff. If this is the case, consider recommending training about the reason for the checkoffs, how the checkoff is designed to improve their performance, and the proper way to use the checkoff.

- Also, you should consider having supervisory observations of procedures being used to make sure that checkoffs are being used correctly.

- If the reason for the checkoff, how the checkoff is designed to improve their performance and the proper way to use the checkoff were well understood, but the checkoff still wasn't used, you should also consider the causes under Management System – SPAC Not Used. If you find a Root Cause in that category, consider the corrective actions listed there to improve the use of checkoffs.

Ideas for Generic Problems:

- If the misuse of checkoffs is a generic problem, consider implementing the corrective actions suggested above on a departmental or site-wide basis.

- Also, consider instituting management / supervisor audits of procedure usage to verify that checkoffs are being used correctly.

References:

- To learn more about improving procedures, attend the 5-Day TapRooT® Advanced Root Cause Analysis Team Leader Training. For more information call (865) 539-2139, or see www.taproot.com/courses.php.

- *Procedure Writing Principles and Practices,* (1998) by Douglas Wieringa, Christopher Moore, and Valerie Barnes, published by Battelle Press, Columbus, Ohio.

misused second check:

Check: You have decided that the problem was at least partially caused by a second check (a formal verification that a task was completed correctly) that was required but was not performed or was performed in a non-independent manner.

Ideas:

- You should consider recommending corrective actions to ensure

Procedures (Followed Incorrectly)

that procedure users properly perform second checks. What type of corrective actions? This depends on the reason that the second check was misused.

- If the second check was misused because the procedure didn't implement second checks well, consider rewriting the procedure. This could include a note at the start of the procedure that explains the purpose of a second check and the proper method to perform one.

- Also, the procedure should clearly call out the need for a second check. An example of a good checkoff is provided below:

	Positioner	Second Checker
7. Close Slurry Outlet Valve (S-23).	_____	_____
8. Check shut the Slurry Dump Valve (S-25).	_____	_____

Note that all checkoffs and second checks are after the steps.

- The checkoff might have been misused because the procedure user didn't understand the reason for the second check, how the second check is designed to improve their performance, and the proper way to perform a second check. If this is the case, consider recommending training for the second checkers and their supervisors about the reason for the second check, how the second check is designed to improve their performance, and the proper way to perform a second check.

- Also, you should consider having supervisory / management observations of second checks being performed to make sure that they are performed correctly.

- If the reason for the second check, how the second check is designed to improve their performance, and the proper way to perform a second check were well understood, but the second check still wasn't performed correctly, you should also consider the causes under Management System – SPAC Not Used. If you find a Root Cause in that category, consider the corrective actions listed there to improve the use of checkoffs.

Ideas for Generic Problems:

- If the performance of second checks is a generic problem, consider implementing the corrective actions suggested above on a departmental or site wide basis.

- Also, consider management / supervisory audits of the performance of second checks to ensure they are being performed correctly.

References:

- To learn more about improving procedures, attend the 5-Day TapRooT® Advanced Root Cause Analysis Team Leader Training. For more information call (865) 539-2139, or see www.taproot.com/courses.php.

- *Procedure Writing Principles and Practices,* (1998) by Douglas Wieringa, Christopher Moore, and Valerie Barnes, published by Battelle Press, Columbus, Ohio.

ambiguous instructions:

Check: You have found that the problem was caused by a procedure that was written so that it could be interpreted in more than one way or that imprecise use of language led to a misinterpretation of the work that was to be performed.

Ideas:

- You should consider recommending that the procedure be rewritten so that it is clear and cannot be misunderstood.

- If words don't seem adequate, incorporate graphics.

- Sometimes a flowchart of the steps, decisions, or process is helpful.

- After the procedure has been revised, test it with several users (with a variety of experience and training) to make sure that they all find it unambiguous.

Ideas for Generic Problems:

- If you find that procedures being ambiguous is a generic problem, then you should consider providing additional guidance for the procedure writers, and you should consider revising the procedure review process to include a specific review for clarity and specificity.

- Once you have trained the procedure writers and revised the review process, then you can review the existing procedures to eliminate any other ambiguity problems.

- Once the ambiguous instructions have been clarified and checked, make sure that you explain the changes to the users.

- This may be a good time to reinforce the actions to be taken if a procedure user finds a problem (like an ambiguous instruction) in a procedure so that the problem can be corrected before an incident occurs.

References:

- To learn more about improving procedures, attend the 5-Day TapRooT® Advanced Root Cause Analysis Team Leader Training.

For more information call (865) 539-2139, or see www.taproot.com/courses.php.

- *Procedure Writing Principles and Practices,* (1998) by Douglas Wieringa, Christopher Moore, and Valerie Barnes, published by Battelle Press, Columbus, Ohio.

equipment identification NI:

Check: You have found that the problem was caused because component/equipment identification or labeling in the field did not agree with the identification in the procedure.

Ideas:

- Consider recommending that the procedure be revised to conform to the field labeling.

- If the field labeling is particularly poor and doesn't agree with the standard user terminology for the equipment, then consider recommending that the field labeling be revised and that the procedure then be revised to match the new field labels.

- It may be a good idea to test the ideas to see if they correct the problem or to seek user feedback before implementing your fix.

- Of course, explain any changes that are made to the users when they are implemented.

Ideas for Generic Problems:

- If you find that there is a generic problem with the procedure not matching the field labels or standard field terminology, you should consider recommending a systematic review of the field and procedure terminology and revise them as appropriate.

- Once the equipment identification problems have been fixed, make sure that you explain the changes to the users.

- This may be a good time to reinforce the actions to be taken if a procedure user finds a problem (like an equipment identification problem) in a procedure so that the problems can be corrected before an incident occurs.

References:

- To learn more about improving procedures, attend the 5-Day TapRooT® Advanced Root Cause Analysis Team Leader Training. For more information call (865) 539-2139, or see www.taproot.com/courses.php.

- *Procedure Writing Principles and Practices,* (1998) by Douglas Wieringa, Christopher Moore, and Valerie Barnes, published by Battelle Press, Columbus, Ohio.

LEVELS 3 – 5: Training

TRAINING

Check: You have decided that the problem was related to training.

Ideas:

- You should continue to analyze the cause of this problem to find the Root Cause of the training problem. You can then correct the Root Causes.

- If you can't identify the Root Causes, then perform a Safeguards Analysis (Chapter 10 of the *TapRooT® Book,* 2008) to identify potential Safeguards that you could add to reduce the likelihood of this problem recurring.

- If part of the problem you are having in analyzing the training is a lack of or incomplete or inaccurate training records, then you should consider recommending improving the training records so that training can be accurately tracked, people missing training can be identified, and continuing training or retraining can be scheduled.

- Be careful that you don't try to use training to fix every problem. For example, you should not expect that all problems or poorly human factored designs can be reliably overcome by providing extensive training to "work-around" poor design or human factors deficiency. Even if you find that training is a substitute for a better designed human-machine interface, consider improving the ergonomics or human factors design of the equipment rather than trying to train the user to work with the bad design.

- Also, you may want to consider recommending that writing (or rewriting) a procedure if a procedure (or a better procedure) would help people successfully complete the work.

- Also, you may want to consider the supervisor's role and the need for better pre-job briefs or walk-thrus before the performing the type of work involved in this problem.

- Also, if you implement an improvement to the training, you should consider how the people who have already been trained will be retrained.

References:

- For more information about the theory behind the systematic approach

Training

to training and developing effective training, we recommend attending the 5-Day TapRooT® Advanced Root Cause Analysis Team Leader Training. For more information about the course call (865) 539-2139, or see www.taproot.com/courses.php.

- *Training in Organizations: Needs Assessment, Development, and Evaluation,* Third Edition (1993) by Irwin Goldstein, published by Brooks/Cole Publishing Company, Pacific Grove, CA.

`No Training` **Check:** You have decided that the problem was caused by a lack of training.

Ideas:

- You should continue to analyze this problem to determine the Root Cause for the lack of training.

- If you can't find the Root Cause for the lack of training, you should still consider recommending the development of effective training for the individual(s) involved to prevent the problem.

Ideas for Generic Problems:

- If you find that the lack of training is more widespread, you should consider recommending effective training for all the workers who need the training to prevent future problems.

- If you find that there is a generic problem with training in that there is no training for other important tasks beyond the one involved in this problem, you should consider recommending a training improvement program that would start with a training needs analysis and a formal decision about which topics need to be included in the training program.

- Once you have implemented the training improvement program, you will need to evaluate the current training status of the workers and develop a remedial training program for those who need it.

References:

- For more information about the theory behind the systematic approach to training and developing effective training, we recommend attending the 5-Day TapRooT® Advanced Root Cause Analysis Team Leader Training. For more information about the course call (865) 539-2139, or see www.taproot.com/courses.php.

- *Training in Organizations: Needs Assessment, Development, and Evaluation,* Third Edition (1993) by Irwin Goldstein, published by Brooks/Cole Publishing Company, Pacific Grove, CA.

Training (No Training)

Check: You have decided that the problem occurred because there was no training offered on the subject because an incomplete task analysis failed to recognize the need for training or because the task was not analyzed. (Task and training needs analysis is the process of listing all tasks or jobs that personnel perform and the requirements or knowledge necessary to successfully perform those tasks.)

Ideas:

- You should consider recommending ways to improve training development and task analysis so that future needs analysis and task analysis are more complete.

- If you don't have any training needs analysis, you should consider developing a more formal training program based on a systematic approach to training.

- If you already use a systematic approach to training, then you need to evaluate why this task was omitted from the task analysis performed before the training development. Consider recommending ways to improve your task analysis.

Ideas for Generic Problems:

- If performing adequate task and needs analysis is a generic problem, you will need to consider recommending analysis or reanalysis of the training needs for all significant job responsibilities.

- Once you have identified all the additional training needed by the workers, you will need to implement a training program to provide additional training to the already qualified workers and revise the initial training program to provide the training that new workers need.

References:

- *Training in Organizations: Needs Assessment, Development, and Evaluation,* Third Edition (1993) by Irwin Goldstein, published by Brooks/Cole Publishing Company, Pacific Grove, CA.

- Attend the 5-Day TapRooT® Advanced Root Cause Analysis Team Leader Training. For more information about the training call (865) 539-2139, or see www.taproot.com/courses.php.

decided not to train:

Check: You have found that there was a conscious decision not to train people on the task that caused this problem.

Training (No Training)

Ideas:

- You should consider recommending the development of effective training on the task that caused this problem.

- If this work is infrequently performed, you should also consider recommending that a pre-job brief or walk-through should be performed before starting the work.

Ideas for Generic Problems:

- If you find that deciding not to train people is a generic problem, then analyze why these inappropriate decisions were made. This may be related to improper task analysis or poor decisions about the need for training. You may want to consider developing written guidance to help people decide which tasks need training and which tasks don't.

- Next, consider recommending a review of the training program focused on past training content decisions. You will be identifying potential additional training needs.

- Once you have identified all the additional training needed by the workers, implement a training program to provide additional training to the already qualified workers and revise the initial training program to provide the training that new workers need.

References:

- For more information about the theory behind the systematic approach to training and developing effective training, we recommend attending the 5-Day TapRooT® Advanced Root Cause Analysis Team Leader Training. For more information about the course call (865) 539-2139, or see www.taproot.com/courses.php.

- *Training in Organizations: Needs Assessment, Development, and Evaluation,* Third Edition (1993) by Irwin Goldstein, published by Brooks/Cole Publishing Company, Pacific Grove, CA.

no learning objective:

Check: You have decided that the problem occurred because there was no training because there were no written learning objectives in lesson plans that address the task(s) involved in the problem.

Ideas:

- You should consider recommending the development of effective training with specific learning objectives that address the problem.

- If you find that a lack of learning objectives is a generic problem, then you should try to find out why the learning objectives were not developed for tasks that were supposed to be included in the training.

Ideas for Generic Problems:

- If you find that the development of learning objectives is a generic problem, then you should consider recommending a review of the training program focused on evaluation of the learning objectives.

- Once you have identified all the additional training (based on the new learning objectives) needed by the workers, you will need to implement a training program to provide additional training to the already qualified workers and revise the initial training program to provide the training that new workers need.

References:

- For more information about the theory behind the systematic approach to training and developing effective training, we recommend attending the 5-Day TapRooT® Advanced Root Cause Analysis Team Leader Training. For more information about the course call (865) 539-2139, or see www.taproot.com/courses.php.

- *Training in Organizations: Needs Assessment, Development, and Evaluation,* Third Edition (1993) by Irwin Goldstein, published by Brooks/Cole Publishing Company, Pacific Grove, CA.

missed required training:

Check: You have decided that the problem occurred because there was no training because the worker did not attend required training.

Ideas:

- You should consider recommending that the person attend the required training. You should consider checking to see if others also miss this or other required training. If they did, this may be a generic problem and you should consider the suggestions under the Ideas for Generic Problems.

- If the training records are not complete enough to determine if people have attended required training, you should consider recommending improvements to the training records system.

Ideas for Generic Problems:

- If others also miss this or other required training, this may be a generic problem. You should look into the reasons that people are not attending required training and fix them. These reasons could include:
  a. Problems with the training scheduling.

b. Problems with student notification.

c. Problems with taking, recording, and tracking attendance (training records).

d. Problems with scheduling and holding make-up training.

e. Poor enforcement of the requirements for training (also consider the Management System - SPAC Not Used Root Causes and corrective actions).

f. Problems with the training requirement policy (also consider the Management System - SPAC NI Root Causes and corrective actions).

g. Problems with the qualification system if people who do not attend required training are still qualified under company policies to perform the work related to the required training.

Understanding NI

Check: You have decided that the problem was caused by the worker not understanding a task, system, a system's response, or other needed information because of faults in the training.

Ideas:

- You need to continue to analyze the problem to find the Root Cause or causes of the training problem.

- If you can't find the Root Cause of the problem, you may consider recommending the development of effective training that includes appropriate learning objectives, classroom delivery, repetition, and testing to see that the skill was acquired.

- Also, you should consider recommending the development and scheduling of continuing training for tasks that are infrequently performed.

Ideas for Generic Problems:

- If you find that understanding of training is a generic problem, you should consider recommending a thorough audit of the training program to find the underlying causes of the program's failure.

- Once you have identified and corrected all the problems with the training program, you should consider recommending a re-deployment of the training program that includes development of new training modules.

- You should also evaluate the training level of people trained in the old training program and recommend retraining as needed.

- Of course, the initial training program will need to be revised with the new training modules to provide the training that new workers need.

Training (Understanding NI)

References:

- For more information about the theory behind the systematic approach to training and developing effective training, we recommend attending the 5-Day TapRooT® Advanced Root Cause Analysis Team Leader Training. For more information about the course call (865) 539-2139, or see www.taproot.com/courses.php.

- *Training in Organizations: Needs Assessment, Development, and Evaluation,* Third Edition (1993) by Irwin Goldstein, published by Brooks/Cole Publishing Company, Pacific Grove, CA.

learning objective NI:

Check: You have decided that the problem occurred because the written learning objectives in the lesson plans failed to ensure that the training provided the knowledge or skill needed to perform the task.

Ideas:

- You should consider recommending an appropriate learning objective and that training be developed for current and future workers to ensure that they develop the skills and knowledge required to perform the task.

- Learning objectives should be "performance based" so that the worker can clearly demonstrate (perform) the knowledge, skills, or abilities that are required.

Ideas for Generic Problems:

- If you decide that poor learning objectives are a generic problem, you should try to determine why the poor learning objectives are being developed and fix the generic problem.

- Once you have fixed the generic problem that causes the learning objective to be inadequate, you should consider recommending that the entire training program be reviewed and the learning objective and training be improved so that the workers learn the skills and knowledge necessary to perform required tasks.

- You should also evaluate the training level of people trained in the old training program and recommend remedial training as needed.

- Of course, the initial training program will need to be revised to include the newly developed learning objectives and training modules.

References:

- For more information about the theory behind the systematic approach to training and developing effective training, we recommend attending the 5-Day TapRooT® Advanced Root Cause Analysis Team Leader

Training. For more information about the course call (865) 539-2139, or see www.taproot.com/courses.php.

- *Training in Organizations: Needs Assessment, Development, and Evaluation,* Third Edition (1993) by Irwin Goldstein, published by Brooks/Cole Publishing Company, Pacific Grove, CA.

lesson plan NI:

Check: You have decided that the problem was caused by lesson plans that didn't ensure effective training.

Ideas:

- You should consider recommending the revision of the lesson plan so that the particular training problem is corrected. This could include:
  - Adding specific material
  - Correcting technical inaccuracies
  - Ensuring that all learning objectives are covered
  - Improving the instructional media
  - Including appropriate reference material or aids
  - Providing improved evaluation methods or materials
  - Developing new instructional techniques

Ideas for Generic Problems:

- If you find that inadequate lesson plans are a generic problem, you need to determine why better lesson plans aren't being developed.

- Once you have fixed the Generic Cause of this problem, you should consider recommending a complete audit of the current lesson plans and improvement of those that need it.

- You should also evaluate the training level of people trained in the old training program and recommend remedial training as needed.

- The initial training program will need to be revised to include the newly developed lesson plans.

References:

- For more information about the theory behind the systematic approach to training and developing effective training, we recommend attending the 5-Day TapRooT® Advanced Root Cause Analysis Team Leader Training. For more information about the course call (865) 539-2139, or see www.taproot.com/courses.php.

- *Training in Organizations: Needs Assessment, Development, and Evaluation,* Third Edition (1993) by Irwin Goldstein, published by Brooks/Cole Publishing Company, Pacific Grove, CA.

Training (Understanding NI)

instruction NI:

Check: You have decided that the problem was caused by inadequate presentation of the training.

Ideas:

- You should consider recommending that the instructional techniques be improved to provide adequate training.

Ideas for Generic Problems:

- If you find that inadequate instructional techniques are a generic problem, consider recommending improvements in the instructor training and evaluation to correct the generic problem.

- Consider recommending enhanced instructor evaluation techniques to ensure that future instruction is frequently and professionally evaluated to guarantee that effective instructional techniques are adhered to and to ensure that continual improvements are made to the quality of instruction.

- Once the generic instruction problems have been corrected, consider recommending the evaluation of current worker knowledge and skills and, where needed, implement retraining for current workers.

References:

- For more information about the theory behind the systematic approach to training and developing effective training, we recommend attending the 5-Day TapRooT® Advanced Root Cause Analysis Team Leader Training. For more information about the course call (865) 539-2139, or see www.taproot.com/courses.php.

- *Training in Organizations: Needs Assessment, Development, and Evaluation,* Third Edition (1993) by Irwin Goldstein, published by Brooks/Cole Publishing Company, Pacific Grove, CA.

practice/repetition NI:

Check: You have decided that the problem was caused by not repeating training enough so that information could be learned (retained in long term memory) and skills practiced.

Ideas:

- Consider recommending that the skill be practiced more extensively or that the training be repeated to ensure that the skill or knowledge is thoroughly mastered.

- To ensure retention, presentation of material up to 9 different times in a variety of settings and instructional techniques is commonly needed.

- Consider recommending more simulator time to develop proficiency.

- Or consider recommending more practice of the task under supervision in the field or control room.

- If the task is infrequently performed, consider developing a job aid to help people remember the information they need to perform the task.

Ideas for Generic Problems:

- If you find that a lack of practice is a generic problem, analyze the training program to determine why more repetition wasn't included in the training program.

- Once you have discovered the Generic Cause of this problem, consider recommending corrective actions to ensure that adequate repetition is included in the development of future training.

- Also, if lack of practice is a generic problem, consider recommending the evaluation of current worker knowledge and skills and, where needed, implementing retraining for current workers.

References:

- For more information about the theory behind the systematic approach to training and developing effective training, we recommend attending the 5-Day TapRooT® Advanced Root Cause Analysis Team Leader Training. For more information about the course call (865) 539-2139, or see www.taproot.com/courses.php.

- *Training in Organizations: Needs Assessment, Development, and Evaluation,* Third Edition (1993) by Irwin Goldstein, published by Brooks/Cole Publishing Company, Pacific Grove, CA.

testing NI:

Check: You have decided that at least one cause for the problem was a failure to detect a lack of skill or knowledge during the testing of a worker.

Ideas:

- You should consider recommending retraining and testing of the worker.

- Also, consider alternative methods for testing that may be more effective in evaluating the knowledge, skills, and abilities required to perform the job. Perhaps a combination of written testing, verbal evaluation, and actual observation of performance in the field might be more effective than written testing or field observation alone.

Ideas for Generic Problems:

- If you find that inadequate testing is a generic problem, analyze the Generic Cause of the inadequate testing and consider recommending improvements to the entire testing program.

- Also, if you find that inadequate testing is a generic problem, re-evaluate the knowledge, skills, and abilities of all current workers and provide additional retraining and retesting as needed.

References:

- For more information about the theory behind the systematic approach to training and developing effective training, we recommend attending the 5-Day TapRooT® Advanced Root Cause Analysis Team Leader Training. For more information about the course call (865) 539-2139, or see www.taproot.com/courses.php.

- *Training in Organizations: Needs Assessment, Development, and Evaluation,* Third Edition (1993) by Irwin Goldstein, published by Brooks/Cole Publishing Company, Pacific Grove, CA.

continuing training NI:

Check: You have decided that the problem was caused by insufficient continuing training of the worker.

Ideas:

- You should consider recommending more frequent continuing training based on the type of work being performed, the frequency at which the work is performed, changes to the work being performed, and the consequences of a mistake.

Ideas for Generic Problems:

- If you find that a lack of continuing training is a generic problem, you will need to analyze the Generic Cause of the problem and consider recommending improvements for the continuing training program.

- Also, consider implementing the improved continuing training as soon as possible to avoid additional incidents.

- In addition, consider developing a job aid (for example, a procedure) to help people remember the information they need to perform the task to reduce the memory requirements.

Training (Understanding NI)

References:

- For more information about the theory behind the systematic approach to training and developing effective training, we recommend attending the 5-Day TapRooT® Advanced Root Cause Analysis Team Leader Training. For more information about the course call (865) 539-2139, or see www.taproot.com/courses.php.

- *Training in Organizations: Needs Assessment, Development, and Evaluation,* Third Edition (1993) by Irwin Goldstein, published by Brooks/Cole Publishing Company, Pacific Grove, CA.

LEVELS 3 – 5: Quality Control

QUALITY CONTROL **Check:** You have decided that the problem was at least partially caused by the failure to perform reasonable inspections, functional tests, or quality verification checks during or after completion of work or because the checks that were performed failed to detect the problem when a reasonable check should have caught it.

Ideas:

- Continue to analyze this problem until you find a Root Cause. You can then correct the Root Causes.

- If you can't identify the Root Causes, then perform a Safeguards Analysis (Chapter 10 of the TapRooT® Book, 2008) to identify potential Safeguards that you could add to reduce the likelihood of this problem recurring.

- Also, consider recommending improved inspections, functional tests, or quality verifications even though you don't know the Root Cause of this problem.

- Be careful that you don't try to use inspections to fix every problem. Instead, you may want to consider other methods to improve quality such as Statistical Process Control (SPC) or re-engineering the work to eliminate the potential for this kind of problem. To start re-engineering the process, first develop a detailed SnapCharT® of the current process, then a chart of the optimized process.

- Also, consider performing a Safeguards Analysis (Chapter 10 of the *TapRooT® Book,* 2008) to identify potential Safeguards that you could add to reduce the likelihood of this problem recurring without requiring an additional QC check.

Quality Control

Ideas for Generic Problems:

- If you decide that QC is a generic problem, then consider recommending corrective actions to eliminate the cause. These corrective actions would depend on the Root Causes.

- One way to start the improvement process for a generic QC problem is to benchmark your QC practices against other facilities with a reputation for highly reliable performance. The goal of the review would be to identify programmatic fixes that would improve your QC process and lead to improved overall performance.

- Also, consider recommending a review of similar work so that other similar work can be improved before a similar, but different, incident occurs.

- If the effort to review the work is extensive because of the number or complexity of the tasks, consider recommending a phased approach by prioritizing the work to be reviewed and addressing the most important tasks first.

References:

- For more information about SPC, read *Understanding Statistical Process Control*, (1992) by Donald J. Wheeler and David S. Chambers and published by SPC Press, Knoxville, TN.

No Inspection — **Check:** You have determined that no inspection was performed when, in your judgment, one should have been.

Ideas:

- You should continue to analyze the cause of this problem to find the Root Cause(s). You can then correct the Root Cause(s).

- If you can't identify the Root Cause(s), then perform a Safeguards Analysis (Chapter 10 of the *TapRooT® Book*, 2008) to identify potential Safeguards that you could add to reduce the likelihood of this problem recurring without requiring an additional QC check.

- Also, you may want to consider recommending improved inspections, functional tests, or quality verifications even though you don't know the Root Cause of this problem.

- Be careful that you don't try to use inspections to fix every problem. Instead, you may want to consider other methods to improve quality such as Statistical Process Control (SPC) or re-engineering the work to eliminate the potential for this kind of problem. To start re-engineering the process, first develop a detailed SnapCharT® of the current process, then a chart of the optimized process.

Quality Control (No Inspection)

Ideas for Generic Problems:

- One way to start the improvement process for a generic inspection problem is to benchmark your inspection practices against other facilities with a reputation for highly reliable performance. The goal of the review would be to identify programmatic fixes that would improve your inspection practices and lead to improved overall performance.

- Also, you should consider recommending a review of similar work so that other similar work inspection can be implemented before a similar, but different, incident occurs.

- If the effort to review the work is extensive because of the number or complexity of the tasks, consider recommending a phased approach by prioritizing the work to be reviewed and addressing the most important tasks first.

References:

- For more information about SPC, read *Understanding Statistical Process Control,* (1992) by Donald J. Wheeler and David S. Chambers and published by SPC Press, Knoxville, TN.

inspection not required:

Check: You have determined that no inspection was performed because an inspection was not required and, in your judgment, one should have been required because of the safety, quality, or production significance of the work.

Ideas:

- Consider recommending a required quality control inspection.

- Also, consider other methods to improve quality such as Statistical Process Control (SPC) or re-engineering the work to eliminate the potential for this kind of problem. To start re-engineering the process, first develop a detailed SnapCharT® of the current process, then a chart of the optimized process.

- Also, you may perform a Safeguards Analysis (Chapter 10 of the *TapRooT® Book,* 2008) to identify potential Safeguards that you could add to reduce the likelihood of this problem recurring without requiring an additional QC check.

Ideas for Generic Problems:

- Consider the Generic Cause of why no inspection was required even though, in your judgment, one should have been required because of the safety, quality, or production significance of the work. If you

Quality Control (No Inspection)

can find a Generic Cause, then you should consider recommending corrective action to eliminate the cause.

- One way to start the improvement process for a generic inspection problem is to benchmark your inspection practices against other facilities with a reputation for highly reliable performance. The goal of the review would be to identify programmatic fixes that would improve your inspection practices and lead to improved overall performance.

- Also, consider recommending a review of similar work so that other similar procedures (that don't have appropriate QC inspections) can be improved before a similar, but different incident occurs.

- If the effort to review and correct these procedures is extensive because of the number or complexity of the procedures, consider recommending a phased approach by prioritizing the procedures and addressing the most important ones first.

References:

- For more information about SPC, read *Understanding Statistical Process Control*, (1992) by Donald J. Wheeler and David S. Chambers and published by SPC Press, Knoxville, TN.

no hold point:

Check: You have determined that a required inspection was not performed because the procedure or work plan did not include an inspection hold point.

Ideas:

- Consider adding a hold point (perhaps with a written release signature) to the appropriate procedure or work plan.

- Also, consider other methods to improve quality such as Statistical Process Control (SPC) or re-engineering the work to eliminate the potential for this kind of problem. To start re-engineering the process, first develop a detailed SnapCharT® of the current process, then a chart of the optimized process.

- You may also perform a Safeguards Analysis (Chapter 10 of the *TapRooT® Book*, 2008) to identify potential Safeguards that you could add to reduce the likelihood of this problem recurring without requiring an additional QC check.

Ideas for Generic Problems:

- Consider the Generic Cause of why the procedure or work plan did not include an inspection hold point. One way to start analyzing the problem would be to perform a detailed analysis of selected "important" procedures and see if these procedures also lacked hold points. If they did, the type of hold point needed could be noted and the scope of the review could be expanded until all procedures that were worthy of review were reviewed.

References:

* For more information about SPC, read *Understanding Statistical Process Control,* (1992) by Donald J. Wheeler and David S. Chambers and published by SPC Press, Knoxville, TN.

hold point not performed:

Check: You have determined that a required inspection was not performed because it was skipped, deleted, ignored, overlooked, or for some other reason not performed.

Ideas:

* If a Root Cause under Management Systems - SPAC Not Used was also selected, consider combining the corrective action into a single corrective action for both Root Causes. Recommendations for improving the use of required policies or procedures are detailed under the Management Systems - SPAC Not Used corrective action suggestions.

* Also, consider other methods to improve quality such as Statistical Process Control (SPC) or re-engineering the work to eliminate the potential for this kind of problem. To start re-engineering the process, first develop a detailed SnapCharT® of the current process, then a chart of the optimized process.

* You may also perform a Safeguards Analysis (Chapter 10 of the *TapRooT® Book,* 2008) to identify potential Safeguards that you could add to reduce the likelihood of this problem recurring without requiring an additional QC check.

Ideas for Generic Problems:

* Consider the Generic Cause of why the hold point was not performed. If you can find a Generic Cause, then consider recommending corrective actions to eliminate the cause.

References:

* For more information about SPC, read *Understanding Statistical Process Control,* (1992) by Donald J. Wheeler and David S. Chambers and published by SPC Press, Knoxville, TN.

Quality Control (No Inspection)

Check: You have decided that the problem was caused by specifying inspection, quality verification, or functional testing that was not adequate or comprehensive enough to detect possible problems and that the inspection or testing needs to be improved.

Ideas:

- You should continue to analyze the cause of this problem to find the Root Cause(s). You can then correct the Root Cause(s).

- If you can't identify the Root Cause(s), then perform a Safeguards Analysis (Chapter 10 of the *TapRooT® Book,* 2008) to identify potential Safeguards that you could add to reduce the likelihood of this problem recurring.

- Also, consider recommending improved inspections, or functional tests, or quality verifications even though you don't know the Root Cause of this problem.

- Be careful that you don't try to use inspections to fix every problem. Instead, consider other methods to improve quality such as Statistical Process Control (SPC) or re-engineering the work to eliminate the potential for this kind of problem. To start re-engineering the process, first develop a detailed SnapCharT® of the current process, then a chart of the optimized process.

Ideas for Generic Problems:

- Consider the Generic Cause of this problem. If you can find a Generic Cause, then you should consider recommending corrective actions to eliminate the cause.

- Also, consider recommending a review of similar work so that other similar work inspection can be implemented before a similar, but different incident occurs.

- If the effort to review the work is extensive because of the number or complexity of the tasks, consider recommending a phased approach by prioritizing the work to be reviewed and addressing the most important tasks first.

References:

- For more information about SPC, read *Understanding Statistical Process Control,* (1992) by Donald J. Wheeler and David S. Chambers and published by SPC Press, Knoxville, TN.

inspection instructions NI:

Check: You have decided that an incident occurred because the quality control instructions need to be improved.

Ideas:

- Consider recommending inspection instructions that would clearly indicate what is to be inspected and how it is to be inspected so that the inspection will detect the problem that caused this incident.

- Also, consider other methods to improve quality such as Statistical Process Control (SPC) or re-engineering the work to eliminate the potential for this kind of problem. To start re-engineering the process, first develop a detailed SnapCharT® of the current process, then a chart of the optimized process.

- You may also perform a Safeguards Analysis (Chapter 10 of the *TapRooT® Book,* 2008) to identify potential Safeguards that you could add to reduce the likelihood of this problem recurring without requiring a QC check.

- Also, this may be a good time to explain to inspectors what they are supposed to do if they find that an inspection instruction is confusing or, in their view, inadequate.

Ideas for Generic Problems:

- Consider the Generic Cause of why the inspection instruction needed improvement. If you can find a Generic Cause, then consider recommending corrective actions to eliminate the cause.

- One way to start the improvement process for an inspection instruction problem is to benchmark your inspection instructions against other facilities with a reputation for highly reliable performance. The goal of the review would be to identify programmatic fixes that would improve your inspection instructions and lead to improved overall performance.
  - Once you have identified good practices, train your staff who writes inspection instructions about the good practices that you have identified and how they should incorporate them into your procedures.
  - Consider institutionalizing these good practices by developing a "how to write procedures and inspection instructions" manual or training course for new employees that write procedures and inspection instructions.
  - Once everyone is trained, consider reviewing all current inspection instructions to determine which ones need to be rewritten to conform to the new good practices.

Quality Control (QC NI)

- If reviewing and rewriting all inspection instructions seems like an excessive amount of work, consider prioritizing the instructions to be reviewed and proposing a reasonable schedule to complete the entire review.

References:

- For more information about SPC, read *Understanding Statistical Process Control,* (1992) by Donald J. Wheeler and David S. Chambers and published by SPC Press, Knoxville, TN.

inspection techniques NI:

Check: You have decided that an incident occurred because the inspection techniques need to be improved.

Ideas:

- Consider improving the inspection techniques or devices so that they can detect the problem that caused this incident.

- Also, consider other methods to improve quality such as Statistical Process Control (SPC) or re-engineering the work to eliminate the potential for this kind of problem. To start re-engineering the process, first develop a detailed SnapCharT® of the current process, then a chart of the optimized process.

- You may also perform a Safeguards Analysis (Chapter 10 of the *TapRooT® Book,* 2008) to identify potential Safeguards that you could add to reduce the likelihood of this problem recurring without requiring a QC check.

- Also, this may be a good time to explain to inspectors what they are supposed to do if they find that an inspection technique is, in their view, inadequate.

Ideas for Generic Problems:

- Consider the Generic Cause of why the inspection technique was inadequate. If you can find a Generic Cause, then consider recommending corrective actions to eliminate the cause.

- One way to start the improvement process for an inspection technique problem is to benchmark your inspection techniques against other facilities with a reputation for highly reliable performance. The goal of the review would be to identify programmatic fixes that would improve your inspection techniques and lead to improved overall performance.
  a. Once you have identified good practices, rewrite your inspection instructions to include the new inspection techniques.

Quality Control (QC NI)

b. Next, train the personnel who perform the inspections in the new techniques.

c. If developing new inspection techniques seems like an excessive amount of work, consider prioritizing the development and improving the most important inspections first.

References:

- For more information about SPC, read *Understanding Statistical Process Control,* (1992) by Donald J. Wheeler and David S. Chambers and published by SPC Press, Knoxville, TN.

foreign material exclusion during work NI:

Check: You have decided that the measures to prevent foreign material and debris from entering undesirable locations (inaccessible or un-inspectable) caused an incident and need to be improved.

Ideas:

- Consider recommending improved methods to prevent foreign material from entering undesirable locations. This can include:
    - using covers to block openings, attaching tools & parts to lanyards so they can't fall
    - covering buttons or loose items on clothes with HP tape
    - wearing clean suits with no loose items
    - taking an inventory of all parts, materials, and tools as they are taken into and out of the work site.
    - using lanyards on covers so they can't be accidentally dropped into the inaccessible locations

- Also, consider conducting the work in an enclosed environment (glove bag or glove box) so that foreign material doesn't contaminate an item being worked on.

Ideas for Generic Problems:

- If you find that foreign material exclusion is a generic problem, consider recommending corrective actions to eliminate the cause.

- Consider developing (or improving) a foreign material exclusion program. One way to start this process is to benchmark your practices against an industry leader with a reputation for excellent performance. Consider visiting a location that performs clean room work to see first hand the practices that are used. Places to visit may include the NASA facilities at Cape Canaveral, a semiconductor manufacturer, or a nuclear plant.

- Once you have improved your foreign material exclusion program, you will need to train all those involved in the new program and let them practice the new techniques.

Quality Control (QC NI)

- You will also need to incorporate this new training into the initial training program for new employees.

COMMUNICATIONS

Check: You have decided that communication between two or more people was a cause of the problem.

Ideas:

- You should continue to analyze the cause of this problem to find the Root Cause(s) of the communications problem. You can then correct the Root Cause(s).

- If you can't identify the Root Cause(s), then perform a Safeguards Analysis (Chapter 10 of the *TapRooT® Book,* 2008) to identify potential Safeguards that you could add to reduce the likelihood of this problem recurring.

References:

- For more information about the theory behind communication, we recommend attending the 5-Day TapRooT® Advanced Root Cause Analysis Team Leader Training. For more information call (865) 539-2139, or see www.taproot.com/courses.php.

- *INPO Good Practice: Operational Communications Verbal:* Institute of Nuclear Power Operations, Atlanta, GA).

- *INPO Good Practice: Shift Relief and Turnover*: Institute of Nuclear Power Operations, Atlanta, GA).

No Comm. or Not Timely

Check: You have decided that the problem was caused by a failure to communicate or by communicating too late.

Ideas:

- You should continue to analyze the cause of this problem to find the Root Cause(s) of the communications problem. You can then correct the Root Cause(s).

- If you can't identify the Root Cause, then perform a Safeguards Analysis (Chapter 10 of the *TapRooT® Book,* 2008) to identify potential Safeguards that you could add to reduce the likelihood of this problem recurring.

- Consider recommending methods to improve and encourage communications even though you don't know the Root Cause of the problem.

References:

- For more information about the theory behind communication we recommend attending the 5-Day TapRooT® Advanced Root Cause Analysis Team Leader Training. For more information call (865) 539-2139, or see www.taproot.com/courses.php.

Communications

- *INPO Good Practice: Operational Communications Verbal*: Institute of Nuclear Power Operations, Atlanta, GA).

comm. system NI:

Check: You have decided that the problem was caused by a failure to communicate because no method or system existed for communicating. (For example: the radio channel became overloaded during an incident and important communications didn't occur.)

Ideas:

- Consider recommending improvements to the communications system to eliminate the problem.

- Also, consider implementing training on communications during emergencies to reduce the system overload until the improved communications system can be installed.

Ideas for Generic Problems:

- If you find that communication methods are a generic problem, you should consider performing an overall, systematic review of the communication requirements during normal operations and emergencies. The information gained can be used to develop a communication system plan and to design the necessary communication system.

- If the requirements for communication seem overwhelming, you might consider redesigning the work process and human-machine interfaces to simplify the communication requirements. The information gained in the systematic review of the communication requirements will be an essential part of this redesign process.

References:

- For more information about the theory behind communication we recommend attending the 5-Day TapRooT® Advanced Root Cause Analysis Team Leader Training. For more information call (865) 539-2139, or see www.taproot.com/courses.php.

late communication:

Check: You have decided that the problem was caused by a failure to communicate because events happened too fast to allow time for communications or because of time constraints that inhibited taking time to communicate.

Ideas:

- Consider recommending improvements to the communication system that makes communications easier so that communicating doesn't conflict with other duties.

- Also, consider ways to change the process to reduce the speed and severity of changes or to reduce the workload of those who should be communicating.

Ideas for Generic Problems:

- If you find that late communications are a generic problem, you should consider performing an overall, systematic review of the communication requirements during normal operations and emergencies and the workload of those required to communicate. The information gained can be used to develop a staffing and communication plan or to redesign the work or the communication system.

- If the requirements for communications or the workload seem overwhelming, you might consider redesigning the work process and human-machine interfaces to simplify the work and the communication requirements. The information gained in the systematic review mentioned above will be an essential part of this redesign process.

References:

- For more information about the theory behind communication we recommend attending the 5-Day TapRooT® Advanced Root Cause Analysis Team Leader Training. For more information call (865) 539-2139, or see www.taproot.com/courses.php.

- *INPO Good Practice: Operational Communications Verbal*: Institute of Nuclear Power Operations, Atlanta, GA).

 Check: You have decided that incorrect, incomplete, or otherwise inadequate turnover of information between personnel during work turnover contributed to the problem.

Ideas:

- You should continue to analyze the problem to find its Root Cause.

- If you can't find the Root Cause of the turnover problem, you may want to consider recommending improved shift or work turnover practices.

- Also, you may perform a Safeguards Analysis (Chapter 10 of the *TapRooT® Book*, 2008) to identify potential Safeguards to reduce the likelihood of this problem recurring.

Ideas for Generic Problems:

- Also, if you find that inadequate turnover is a generic problem, then you should consider developing an internal good practice on turnover and training of the workers about the improved turnover practices.

- You should also consider implementing supervisor and management audits/assessments of field turnovers to reinforce the good practices.

References:

- *INPO Good Practice: Shift Relief and Turnover:* Institute of Nuclear Power Operations, Atlanta, GA).

- Department of Energy Standard 1038, *Guide to Good Practices for Operations Turnover,* DOE-STD-1038-93, (June 1993). This is available on DOE's Office of Scientific and Technical Information (OSTI) web site at: www.osti.gov/servlets/purl/296701-qDsL7Y/webviewable/

- For more information about the theory behind communication, we recommend attending the 5-Day TapRooT® Advanced Root Cause Analysis Team Leader Training. For more information call (865) 539-2139, or see www.taproot.com/courses.php.

no standard turnover process:

Check: You have decided that if a standard turnover process existed and was used, the problem would not have happened.

Ideas:

- Consider recommending the development of a standard turnover process for individuals, shifts, or perhaps turnover of work when people change jobs.

- Consider including a written, formal turnover that includes consistent, specific information.

- Once you have developed a standard turnover process, consider recommending training for the workers on the process. This training should include how the standard turnover process will improve performance.

- Also, consider recommending supervision and management audits of the turnovers in the field to reinforce the standard and the lessons learned in training.

Ideas for Generic Problems:

- Establishing a standard turnover process should address the generic problem. However, you could also consider adopting the standard turnover process across the entire facility or across the entire company.

Communications (Turnover NI)

References:

- *INPO Good Practice: Shift Relief and Turnover:* Institute of Nuclear Power Operations, Atlanta, GA).

- Department of Energy Standard 1038, *Guide to Good Practices for Operations Turnover*, DOE-STD-1038-93, (June 1993). This is available on DOE's Office of Scientific and Technical Information (OSTI) web site at: www.osti.gov/servlets/purl/296701-qDsL7Y/webviewable/

turnover process not used:

Check: You have found that a standard turnover process existed, but that the problem occurred because the process was not used.

Ideas:

- If the turnover process was not required to be used, you should consider developing a policy requiring the use of the standard turnover process.

- Once this policy is in place, make sure that all workers are trained about the process, the requirement to use it, and how the process will improve their performance.

- If the turnover process was required to be used but wasn't used, look into the reasons it wasn't used and correct the causes. You may find more information about the reasons for the policy being violated under the Management System – SPAC Not Used section of the tree. For example, if a formal, standard, written turnover was required, but no time was allowed for turnover between shifts, consider including a 30 minute paid overlap between shifts to provide time for a formal turnover.

- Once the corrective action is in place, make sure that all workers are trained about the changes and how the changes will improve their performance.

Ideas for Generic Problems:

- The above corrective actions should address the generic problem. However, you could also consider implementing them across the entire facility or across the entire company.

References:

- *INPO Good Practice: Shift Relief and Turnover:* Institute of Nuclear Power Operations, Atlanta, GA).

- Department of Energy Standard 1038, *Guide to Good Practices for Operations Turnover*, DOE-STD-1038-93, (June 1993). This is available on DOE's Office of Scientific and Technical Information (OSTI) web site at: www.osti.gov/servlets/purl/296701-qDsL7Y/webviewable/

- For more information about the theory behind communication, we recommend attending the 5-Day TapRooT® Advanced Root Cause Analysis Team Leader Training. For more information call (865) 539-2139, or see www.taproot.com/courses.php.

turnover process NI:

Check: You have decided that deficiencies in the standard turnover process were at least partially responsible for the problem.

Ideas:

- You should consider recommending improvements for the standard turnover process to prevent recurrence of the problem. This may include developing a standard turnover checklist, including additional items on a checklist, or providing sufficient paid time for shift turnover to be performed.

- Once you have improved the standard turnover process, train the workers on the process, including the reasons for the improvements (how it will improve performance).

- Also, consider recommending supervision and management audits of the turnovers in the field to reinforce the standard and the lessons learned in training.

Ideas for Generic Problems:

- The above corrective actions should address the generic problem. However, consider implementing them across the entire facility or across the entire company.

References:

- *INPO Good Practice: Shift Relief and Turnover:* Institute of Nuclear Power Operations, Atlanta, GA).

- Department of Energy Standard 1038, *Guide to Good Practices for Operations Turnover,* DOE-STD-1038-93, (June 1993). This is available on DOE's Office of Scientific and Technical Information (OSTI) web site at: www.osti.gov/servlets/purl/296701-qDsL7Y/webviewable/

- For more information about the theory behind communication, we recommend attending the 5-Day TapRooT® Advanced Root Cause Analysis Team Leader Training. For more information call (865) 539-2139, or see www.taproot.com/courses.php.

- *Guide to Good Practices for Logkeeping,* DOE Standard DOE-STD-1035-93 (December 1998), U.S. Department of Energy. This is available on DOE's

Office of Scientific and Technical Information (OSTI) web site at: http://www.osti.gov/bridge/servlets/purl/296714-EIhW8j/webviewable/

Misunderstood Verbal Comm.

Check: You have decided that the problem was caused by misunderstood verbal communications.

Ideas:

- You should continue to analyze the problem to find its Root Cause. You should be sensitive to foreign languages and the impact of accents or dialects.

- If you can't find the Root Cause of the communications problem, you may want to consider recommending practices to improve the verbal communications.

- Also, you may perform a Safeguards Analysis (Chapter 10 of the *TapRooT® Book*, 2008) to identify potential Safeguards that you could add to reduce the likelihood of this problem recurring. One potential Safeguard to verbal communications errors is written communications (procedures and work orders).

Ideas for Generic Problems:

- If you find that errors in verbal communications are a generic problem, then you should consider developing an effective communications course to teach improved communication practices.

- You should also consider implementing supervisor and management audits/assessments of field communications to reinforce the good practices taught in the course.

References:

- For more information about the theory behind communication, we recommend attending the 5-Day TapRooT® Advanced Root Cause Analysis Team Leader Training. For more information call (865) 539-2139, or see www.taproot.com/courses.php.

- *INPO Good Practice: Operational Communications Verbal:* Institute of Nuclear Power Operations, Atlanta, GA).

- *Guide to Good Practices for Communications,* DOE Standard DOE-STD-1031-92 (December 1998), U.S. Department of Energy. This is available on DOE's Office of Scientific and Technical Information (OSTI) web site at: http://www.osti.gov/bridge/servlets/purl/308016-ESMfGf/webviewable/

Check: You have decided that the problem was caused by the failure to use standard terminology.

Ideas:

- If the facility required the use of standard terminology, had trained the workers in its use and the theory behind effective communications and the ways that using standard terminology can improve performance, and had audits of communications in the field, but the individual still didn't use standard terminology, you should consider recommending the solutions under the Management System - SPAC Not Used section of the tree.

- If the facility does NOT have standard terminology that is used for operations and maintenance, then consider recommending the development of standard terminology and training of the workers in the use of standard terminology. The training should include the theory behind effective communications and the ways that using standard terminology can improve performance.

- If the facility had standard terminology but the standard terminology was not used, consider developing a policy requiring the use of standard terminology and the training of the workers in the use of standard terminology. The training should include the theory behind effective communications and the ways that using standard terminology can improve performance.

- Next consider recommending management and supervision audits/ assessments of field communications to reinforce the good practices taught in the course.

Ideas for Generic Problems:

- The above corrective actions should address the generic problem. However, you could also consider implementing them across the entire facility or across the entire company.

References:

- For more information about the theory behind communication, we recommend attending the 5-Day TapRooT® Advanced Root Cause Analysis Team Leader Training. For more information call (865) 539-2139, or see www.taproot.com/courses.php.

- INPO Good Practice: Operational Communications Verbal, (Author & Publisher: Institute of Nuclear Power Operations, Atlanta, GA).

Communications (Misunderstood Verbal Comm.)

standard terminology NI:

Check: You have decided that standard terminology contributed to a communication problem and that to eliminate the problem the standard terminology needs to be improved.

Ideas:

- Consider ways to improve the standard terminology so that it does not cause misunderstandings. This may include eliminating:
  a. Words that sound alike
  b. Words that look alike
  c. Words that are difficult to pronounce or are frequently mispronounce
  d. The use of words that cause confusion because they have more than one meaning
  e. The use of words that not generally understood by the workforce

- Consider getting the workers involved in developing the new standard terminology. Their ideas can help make the terminology more useful and accepted by the workforce.

- Once you have developed the new standard terminology, provide training for the users so that they adopt the new terminology and stop using the old terminology. This change of old habits will be difficult. You will need to provide good reasons why adopting the new terminology is important or the workforce may not make the effort required to change their vocabulary. They will need practice and reinforcement of the new terminology.

- Because changing the words that are used to communicate is difficult, consider an audit/observation program to make sure that the new terminology is adopted.

Ideas for Generic Problems:

- If there are problems similar to those listed below with a large fraction of the facilities standard terminology, there is probably a generic problem with standard terminology. You should consider revising the standard terminology to eliminate or reduce the problems. Problems to look for include words that:
  a. Sound alike
  b. Look alike
  c. Are difficult to pronounce or are frequently mispronounced
  d. Cause confusion because they have more than one meaning
  e. Words that not generally understood by the workforce

- Get workers involved in creating and reviewing these changes in standard terminology.

- Once you have developed the new standard terminology, provide training for the users so that they adopt the new terminology and stop using the old terminology. This change of old habits will be difficult. You will need to provide good reasons why adopting the new terminology is important or the workforce may not make the effort required to change their vocabulary. They will need practice and reinforcement of the new terminology.

- Because changing the words that are used to communicate is difficult, consider an audit/observation program to make sure that the new terminology is adopted.

References:

- Consider reading *INPO Good Practice: Operational Communications Verbal*: Institute of Nuclear Power Operations, Atlanta, GA).

- For more information about the theory behind communication, we recommend attending the 5-Day TapRooT® Advanced Root Cause Analysis Team Leader Training. For more information call (865) 539-2139, or see www.taproot.com/courses.php.

repeat back not used:

Check: You have decided that the problem was caused by not using repeat backs during communications.

Ideas:

- If the facility required the use of repeat backs, had trained the workers in the use of repeat backs and the theory behind effective communications and the ways that using repeat backs can improve performance, and had audits of communications in the field, but the individual still didn't use repeat backs, you should consider recommending the solutions under the Management System - SPAC Not Used section of the tree.

- If the facility does NOT have a requirement to use repeat backs for verbal communications during operations and maintenance, then consider recommending the development of a standard for repeat backs and training of the workers in the use of repeat backs. The training should include the theory behind effective communications and the ways that using repeat backs can improve performance.

- If the facility had a requirement to use repeat backs but a repeat back was not used, you should consider developing training for the workers in the use of repeat backs. The training should include the theory behind effective communications and the ways that repeat backs can improve performance.

- In either of the above cases, consider starting management and supervision audits/assessments of field communications to reinforce the use of repeat backs.

Ideas for Generic Problems:

- The above corrective actions should address the generic problem. However, you could also consider implementing them across the entire facility or across the entire company.

References:

- For more information about the theory behind communication we recommend attending the 5-Day TapRooT® Advanced Root Cause Analysis Team Leader Training. For more information call (865) 539-2139, or see www.taproot.com/courses.php.

- *INPO Good Practice: Operational Communications Verbal:* Institute of Nuclear Power Operations, Atlanta, GA).

long message:

Check: You have decided that the problem was caused by miscommunication that resulted from a loss of information because of a long message.

Ideas:

- Consider recommending improved communications techniques including shortening of messages and replacing long messages with work orders and procedures.

- If the facility had trained the workers in the use of good communications practices, the theory behind effective communications, and the ways that using good communications practices can improve performance, and had audits of communications in the field, but the individual still didn't use repeat backs, consider recommending the solutions under the Management System - SPAC Not Used section of the tree and the Training - Understanding NI section of the tree.

Ideas for Generic Problems:

- If communications that include long messages are a generic problem, then you should consider recommending training on effective communications practices to managers, supervisors, and workers. This training would include the theory behind good communications, the ways that short messages and written communications can improve performance, and practice in developing and delivering effective verbal communications.

- Next, start management and supervision audits/assessments of field communications to reinforce the use of good communications practices.

References:

- For more information about the theory behind communication, we recommend attending the 5-Day TapRooT® Advanced Root Cause Analysis Team Leader Training. For more information call (865) 539-2139, or see www.taproot.com/courses.php.

- *INPO Good Practice: Operational Communications Verbal*: Institute of Nuclear Power Operations, Atlanta, GA).

noisy environment:

Check: You have decided that a message or instruction was misunderstood because of noise interference for the listener.

Ideas:

- Consider reducing the noise in the area. This could include restricting admittance to a control room (reduce the number of people talking and making noise), installing quieter cooling fans in equipment, isolating noisy printers or other pieces of equipment, installing sound deadening panels or ceiling tiles and carpeting, reducing the use of paging systems, reducing the volume of alarms, adding sound barriers to walls, adding more "hear-here" stations for radio or telephone communications, or adding active noise and vibration reduction systems.

- Also, people will need to be trained on the effects of noise on communications and what they need to do if they find an area where they need to communicate that they think is too noisy.

Ideas for Generic Problems:

- If a noisy environment is a generic problem, consider conducting a noise survey and then implementing correct actions as needed to reduce the noise and improve communications.

References:

- For more information about the theory behind communication, we recommend attending the 5-Day TapRooT® Advanced Root Cause Analysis Team Leader Training. For more information call (865) 539-2139, or see www.taproot.com/courses.php.

- *INPO Good Practice: Operational Communications Verbal*: Institute of Nuclear Power Operations, Atlanta, GA).

MANAGEMENT SYSTEM

Check: You have decided that the problem was at least partially caused by a Management System cause. This could include inadequate (confusing, incomplete, unclear, ambiguous, not strict enough) standards, policies, directives, organizational effectiveness, strategic planning, or administrative controls; failure to use existing policies or procedures; inadequate implementation of policy or directives; inadequate audits or failure to perform audits or evaluations; a culture of expediency that placed raw production numbers over quality of work and safety; a failure to transmit management's concerns for quality workmanship and safety; employee concerns that failed to reach the attention of a management level that could, and was willing to, initiate effective corrective actions; the failure of an audit or self-assessment program to find a problem before it becomes an incident; or the failure to develop and implement corrective actions for known malfunctions or deficiencies.

Ideas:

- You should continue to analyze the cause of this problem to find the Root Cause of the Management System problem. You can then correct the Root Causes.

- If you can't identify the Root Causes, then perform a Safeguards Analysis (Chapter 10 of the *TapRooT® Book,* 2008) to identify potential Safeguards that you could add to reduce the likelihood of this problem recurring.

- To develop improved Management Systems you should become familiar with applicable government regulations, industry standards, company policies, and industry good practices that apply to the work being performed.

References:

- *AS/NZS 4801:2001: Occupational health and safety management systems - Specification with guidance for use* www.saiglobal.com/shop/script/details.asp?DocN=AS910602987158

- *AS/NZS 4804:2001: Occupational health and safety management systems - General guidelines* www.saiglobal.com/shop/script/details.asp?DocN=AS694960756228

- Australian Safety Standard Handbook HB 205-2004: *OHS Risk Management Handbook* www.saiglobal.com/shop/script/details.asp?DocN=AS0733757693AT

- *Strategic Management of Health Care Organizations,* (2007) by Linda Swayne et al, published by Wiley.

- *The First-Time Manager,* (2005) by Loren Belker and Gary Topchik, published by AMACOM.

- *1001 Ways to Reward Employees,* (2005) by Bob Nelson, published by Workman Publishing

Standards, Policies, or Admin Controls (SPAC) NI

Check: You have decided that to prevent future problems, your standards, policies, or administrative controls need to be improved.

Ideas:

- You should continue to analyze the cause of this problem to find the Root Cause of the Management System – SPAC NI problem. You can then correct the Root Causes.

- If you can't identify the Root Causes, then perform a Safeguards Analysis (Chapter 10 of the *TapRooT® Book,* 2008) to identify potential Safeguards that you could add to reduce the likelihood of this problem recurring.

- To develop improved standards, policies, or administrative controls, become familiar with applicable government regulations, industry standards, company policies, and industry good practices that apply to the work being performed. You can then develop SPAC that adequately defines the performance required to meet safety, health, environmental, production, maintenance, reliability, and quality objectives.

no SPAC:

Check: You have decided that a standard, policy, or administrative control needs to be developed to prevent this type of problem.

Ideas:

- You should consider recommending an improved SPAC that will reduce the likelihood of this kind of problem occurring in the future.

- To develop an effective SPAC, have a clear objective (outcome) for the work that is being performed.

- Next, review applicable government regulations, industry standards, company policies, or industry good practices that apply to the work.

- Then develop a system or process that ensures that all regulations are met and the objective is accomplished.

- Then document this system or process including specific requirements for workers, supervision, staff, and management.

- The standard should be written in clear, simple, and unambiguous terms.

- Once you have developed the SPAC, communicate it to all involved. This will probably require training.

- Also, consider implementing an audit or assessment program to periodically check compliance with the new SPAC.

Ideas for Generic Problems:

- If the lack of SPAC is a generic problem, then you should consider recommending an assessment of the current management controls and the development of a comprehensive set of SPAC to define management expectations and regulatory requirements.

- You should then recommend training about the new SPAC for all those impacted by the new SPAC. This training should include the reason for the new SPAC and the improvement in performance that is expected.

- Once these new SPAC have been communicated, consider adding them to your periodic audit/assessment program.

not strict enough:

Check: You have decided that the SPAC needs to be made more strict to reduce the likelihood of a problem.

Ideas:

- Consider recommending a modification to the SPAC so that it more exactly and strictly defines the requirements that meet management's expectations and legal requirements.

- Be sure that you review applicable government regulations, industry standards, company policies, or industry good practices when developing the requirements needed in the SPAC.

- If your management's expectations are unclear or not strict enough, develop a compelling case to demonstrate to management the need for them to adopt stricter requirements. You can't expect a management policy to be effective unless management actually believes that it is needed.

- Once you have developed the new, stricter SPAC, you will need to communicate the new SPAC to the all affected personnel (managers, supervisors, workers, contractors, etc).

- Also, consider implementing audits or assessments to check that the SPAC is being used effectively.

Ideas for Generic Problems:

- If you find that not strict enough SPAC is a generic problem, you should consider recommending an assessment of the current management controls to evaluate if they are strict enough.

- Again, if you find that your management's expectations are unclear or not strict enough, you will need to develop a compelling case to demonstrate to management the need for them to adopt stricter requirements.

- You will then recommend changes to the SPAC that need to be made stricter.

- All improved SPAC would need to be communicated and considered for addition to your periodic audit/assessment program.

confusing or incomplete:

Check: You have decided that the SPAC needs to be made clearer or more complete to reduce the likelihood of a problem in the future.

Ideas:

- You should consider recommending a modification to the SPAC so that it more exactly defines the requirements that meet management's expectations and legal requirements.

- Be sure that you review applicable government regulations, industry standards, corporate policies, or industry good practices when developing the requirements needed in the SPAC.

- If your management's expectations are confusing or incomplete, develop a compelling case to demonstrate to management the need for them to clarify and/or detail their requirements. You can't expect a management policy to be clear and complete if management's requirements are confusing and incomplete.

- Once you have developed the clearer and/or more complete SPAC, communicate the new SPAC to the workers.

- Also, consider implementing audits or assessments to check that the SPAC is being used effectively.

Ideas for Generic Problems:

- If you find that confusing or incomplete SPAC is a generic problem, consider recommending an assessment of the current management controls to evaluate their effectiveness.

- Again, if you find that your management's expectations are unclear or incomplete, develop a compelling case to demonstrate to management the need for them to clarify and detail their requirements. You will then recommend changes to the SPAC that need to be improved.

- All improved SPAC would need to be communicated and considered for addition to your periodic audit/assessment program.

technical error:

Check: You have decided that a technical error in the SPAC needs to be corrected to solve this problem.

Ideas:

- You should consider recommending a modification to the SPAC to correct the technical error.

- Once you have corrected the technical error in the SPAC, communicate the correction to the SPAC to all affected (managers, supervisors, workers, contractors, etc).

- Also, this might be a good time to emphasize to the workers what they should do if they think that they have found a technical error in the SPAC.

Ideas for Generic Problems:

- If you find that technical errors in the SPAC are a generic problem, consider recommending an assessment of the technical basis of the SPAC. You can then recommend corrections to the SPAC as needed.

- Then communicate to all affected (managers, supervisors, workers, contractors, etc.) the effort to correct the SPAC, the reasons why accurate SPAC are important to good human performance, and the specifics of the corrections that were made.

drawings/prints NI:

Check: You have decided that drawings or prints need to be improved to prevent this problem from recurring.

Ideas:

- You should consider recommending improvements to the drawings to correct mistakes or enhance their usability.

- Once you have improved the drawings/prints, communicate the improvements to all affected (managers, supervisors, workers, contractors, etc).

- Also, this might be a good time to emphasize to the workers what they should do if they think that the prints are wrong or hard to use.

Ideas for Generic Problems:

- If you find that bad drawings and prints are a generic problem, you should consider recommending changes to improve the process used to develop, revise, and review drawings and prints. This may include training for the people producing the prints in ways that they could make the prints more usable in the field. Improve reviews or walk-downs of prints to verify their accuracy when they are initially produced and on a periodic basis thereafter.

- Also, if the drawings or prints needed improvement because changes had not been incorporated, review the Management of Change process (program to ensure that changes are properly implemented and don't introduce risk) to identify areas for improvement.

- Next, consider implementing a design basis update program where the entire design of your facility would be reviewed and documented and all your prints, drawings, technical documentation, procedures, and training would be updated.

| SPAC Not Used | **Check:** You have decided that standards, policies, or administrative controls that would have prevented or minimized this type of problem were not used. |

Ideas:

- You should continue to investigate why the SPAC was not used. Once you have identified the Root Cause, you can develop effective corrective action.

- If you can't identify the Root Cause, you should consider two options.
  a. Decide if the SPAC was not being used by people other than the person involved in this incident. If others could have had the same type of incident or if the SPAC is occasionally (or frequently) not used by others, then review the SPAC to determine:
    1. If the SPAC is known to the work force and if they understand the reasoning behind the SPAC;
    2. What the rewards and punishment are that enforce the SPAC. The rewards and punishment include the "official" policy and the unofficial rewards system.

  For example, a driver is both rewarded and punished for the speed he drives. If he drives faster than the speed limit, he is rewarded by getting to the destination sooner. If he is caught by the police, he may be punished by a ticket, fine, and higher insurance costs. The reward is soon, certain, and positive. The punishment is delayed, uncertain, and negative. Soon, certain, positive rewards almost always have more influence on behavior than delayed, uncertain, and negative punishments.

Therefore, if you find that your rewards system is rewarding the wrong behavior by frequently providing soon, certain, positive rewards for breaking the rules and infrequently providing delayed, uncertain, and negative punishments when people have an incident, then you need to change the system (see SPAC Not Used, enforcement NI).

b. The second option is that the SPAC was not used and none of the Root Causes listed was present and you find that the person performing the work is the only person in the work force not following the rule. In this case, consider using your company's discipline system.

Many companies have a "progressive" discipline system that starts with formal warnings and gradually escalates to firing the individual if they can't eventually comply with company policy. The system should be well documented and the reason for using it should be well understood.

In this case the reason for using the discipline system needs to be communicated so that people understand that the discipline was not because of the incident, but rather it was because the individual consciously chose to violate a well documented, well understood, generally well followed rule and that the punishment was intended to change the individual's behavior because they had not responded to the rewards that the rest of the work force responds to.

If the individual has repeatedly been disciplined for failure to follow generally well followed rules and the individual is fired as a result of not following a rule that caused an incident, then the whole history of the poor performance and the specific progressive discipline taken needs to be well documented and communicated to the rest of the work force. You should make sure that human resources/labor relations and legal are consulted before official action or communication is initiated.

- Consider taking this opportunity to communicate to the rest of the work force the SPAC, the reason for the SPAC, and the problems that were caused in this particular incident when the SPAC was not followed. This will probably require training.

- Also, consider implementing an audit or assessment program to periodically check compliance with the SPAC that was not followed to make sure that the SPAC is generally being used properly.

Ideas for Generic Problems:

- If not using SPAC is a generic problem, you need to consider an assessment of the current management controls to determine the Root Causes of the failure to follow the SPAC and correct the Root Causes. The start of this assessment should probably be a thorough audit of the Management System and a Root cause analysis of the problems that are discovered.

References:

- For more information about how to audit the use of SPAC: Read Chapter 4 of the *TapRooT® Book*, (2008) for a description of how to use TapRooT® proactively. Call System Improvements at (865) 539-2139 to get assistance with the audit.

communication of SPAC NI:

Check: You have decided that the SPAC was not followed because the communication of the SPAC needs to be improved.

Ideas:

- You should consider improving communication of the SPAC. This could include training for the work force, supervisors, and managers about the SPAC, the reasons for the SPAC's development, how the SPAC improves performance, how not following the SPAC, in this instance, caused problems, and the rewards and punishments that will be used in the future to encourage use of the SPAC.

- Consider using audits, self-assessments, or other reviews to repeatedly reinforce the training and evaluate the effectiveness of the communication of the SPAC.

- DO NOT discipline workers who did not follow a SPAC that was not communicated to them.

Ideas for Generic Problems:

- If communication of SPAC is a generic problem, then review your management controls training program and consider correcting the Root Causes of the problems you identify.

- Consider developing a periodic auditing program to assess the understanding of and compliance with SPAC.

recently changed:

Check: You have decided that SPAC was not followed because the SPAC had been recently changed.

Ideas:

- Changing SPAC requires training to communicate the change plus practice to overcome old habits (the old SPAC).

- You should review the level of knowledge of the new SPAC and the amount of confusion that exists about it.

- You should then consider recommending, as needed, additional training about the new SPAC and practice (under supervision if significant hazard is involved) until the new SPAC is clearly understood and the old practices are replaced by the new SPAC.

Ideas for Generic Problems:

- If changing the SPAC is a generic problem, consider why you are changing so many SPAC.

- If you are constantly changing SPAC, consider a more systematic review of the SPAC and a one time, well documented, well implemented change.

- If your training about changes in SPAC is consistently poor or the practice to learn the new SPAC is insufficient, then you should find the Root Causes of your training program deficiencies and consider implementing improvements.

- Also, review your Management of Change program and see if it was used appropriately and why, if it was, this change was not implemented more effectively.

- Once you've developed improvement recommendations, this might be a good opportunity to reemphasize your Management of Change program (the formal way you implement change) and how it might have prevented problems in this particular incident.

- Also, explain what workers are supposed to do if they have any confusion about new or changed SPAC.

enforcement NI:

Check: You have decided that the SPAC was not used because enforcement of the SPAC needs to be improved.

Ideas:

- This topic is the longest because it is the most frequently misapplied root cause and corrective action. Read all of it before you start developing your corrective action.

- Often a SPAC is not used because:
    - the enforcement is lax;
    - failure to follow the SPAC goes uncorrected;

- noncompliance is accepted by supervision;
- there are no positive incentives to follow the SPAC;
- positive incentives are only infrequently applied;
- unintentional positive incentives are given to violate the SPAC;
- conflicting positive and negative incentives are used (management sometimes rewards people for the same behaviors that they would at other times punish people for); or
- enforcement is seen as inconsistent by the employees.

- One of the first things to consider is whether this is a relatively widespread problem (there are several instances of this problem), or is this a single individual making his own personal choice. If only one person is involved (proven by numerous interviews and no evidence to the contrary), then this is not an enforcement problem. Be careful here. Do not make the assumption that this is an isolated incident without thoroughly investigating the possibility that others are also not following the policy without your knowledge. Ask plenty of questions, and make an honest assessment of the answers. It is here that an investigator can bias the investigation by blaming the employee for a problem, when in reality it is common practice for other employees to also disregard the same policy. In this case, you need to implement a generic corrective action or nothing will change.

- Once you have determined that the enforcement of the SPAC needs improvement, you need to change the rewards system to encourage the behaviors that you want to see. There are two principles that must be considered whenever you are trying to determine how to change people's behaviors.

First of all, you must understand that the method in which the reward is given will determine how your employees react to that reward. There is an Enforcement Spectrum that describes these types of rewards:

If the consequence of the reward is:	Late Uncertain Negative	Soon Certain Negative	Soon Certain Positive
The result will be:	**Non-compliance**	**Reluctant Compliance**	**Committed Behavior**
	Employees will find reasons NOT to follow the policy, and many times will not.	Employees will follow the policy because they HAVE to, not because they WANT to.	Employees WANT to follow the policy, and look for reasons to comply.
	This is the standard discipline system with poor results.	This causes fast change, but employees are not committed.	Most effective. Requires continued effort and creativity.

Your goal when you develop a corrective action is to make the reward for following the policy *SOON, CERTAIN* and *POSITIVE*. Wouldn't it be great if your employees ASKED to follow the policies, instead of finding ways around them!

The second idea when developing corrective actions to change people's behavior is to realize that there are four main motivators that describe why people make the decisions that they do. These motivators are *Time, Effort, Enforcement,* and *Bonus.* Let's take a look at an example of what this means.

During the start-up of a steam turbine, the operator forgets to open one drain valve. This simple mistake results in significant damage to the turbine. The simplified SnapCharT® of this incident is shown here:

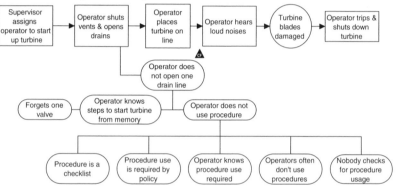

When analyzing this Causal Factor, one of the Root Causes is found to be *enforcement NI.* This is because other operators also disregard the checklist. We need to enforce the use of the turbine start-up checklist by all of our operators. But how can we write an effective corrective action if we don't know why the operators decide not to use the procedure? We need to look at the four motivators to discover why the operators made the rational decision to not use the procedure. By asking questions about these motivators, we can find new information about the incident:

Motivators	Old Behavior: **Does not use checklist**
Time	Saves time, because valves are not physically arranged in the same order as seen in the checklist. Also, the checklist is stored in the Ops Building,, not the Turbine Building.
Effort	Same as Time.
Enforcement	We don't monitor for use of the checklists, but the supervisor yells at the operators if the turbine is not started up quickly.
Bonus	Breaks are longer with quicker start-ups. Also, the operator is seen as experienced, since he can start up the turbine without a checklist.

By taking this information into account, and remembering to incorporate the soon-certain-positive ideas into our thinking, we can now write effective corrective actions. For example:

Motivators	Old Behavior: Does not use checklist	New Behavior: Operators want to use checklist	Soon/Certain/ Positive?
Time	Saves time, because valves are not physically arranged in the same order as seen in the checklist. Also, the checklist is stored in the Ops Building, not the Turbine Building.	- Re-write procedure to have valves in order that the operator expects to operate them - Keep a copy of the checklist right next to the turbine	- Immediately saves time, every time. Start-up takes the same amount of time whether using procedure or not. No longer a time motivation to disregard the procedure.
Effort	Same as Time.	- Start-up not complete until completed copy of checklist is signed and turned in to supervisor	- Now, same amount of effort to use procedure as not.
Enforcement	We don't monitor for use of the checklists, but the supervisor yells at the operators if the turbine is not started up quickly.	- Supervisor audits of checklist usage - Clear discipline policy followed - Supervisors expect checklist usage, no yelling	This is definitely soon (if caught not using checklist during audit), positive and certain, in that no longer yelled at for slower start-up.
Bonus	Breaks are longer with quicker start-ups. Also, the operator is seen as experienced, since he can start up the turbine without a checklist.	- Auditor gives lottery ticket when operator is using checklist correctly	Soon and positive. Doesn't happen every time, but certain to happen if noted.

Note that none of these corrective actions will guarantee compliance by all operators at all times. However, the likelihood that they will use the procedure has increased dramatically.

The Bonus motivator can often be a tough corrective action to figure out. Some "old-school" supervisors complain, "Why should I give a lottery ticket to an operator for doing what he is paid to do in the first place?" While this seems to be a logical question at first glance, it should be understood

Management System (SPAC Not Used)

that there are other rewards besides just monetary rewards. For example, how far does a sincere "Good job" and a pat on the back go, especially if given by the immediate supervisor? Although your employee may say, "yeah, whatever," in reality, people want to be acknowledged for doing a good job. That acknowledgement can take many forms; it is up to you to decide how this fits into your company culture. Bob Nelson's *1001 Ways to Reward Employees* has some great ideas on both monetary and non-monetary reward systems that can make a dramatic effect on employee motivation.

Now that we understand what motivates people to either follow a policy or disregard that policy and make mistakes, let's look at another example. At our delivery company, we have had a rash of traffic tickets and vehicle accidents. We investigate this problem with the four motivators in mind. We find that a driver is both rewarded and punished for the speed he drives. If he drives faster than the speed limit, he is rewarded by getting to the destination sooner. You may even further reinforce this "bad" behavior by punishing drivers who make late deliveries (encouraging them to speed if they get behind schedule). You may even reinforce this bad behavior more by scheduling too much work so that the only way to stay on schedule is to speed. Finally, you may also continue to reinforce this bad behavior by rewarding the drivers with the best on-time delivery record. However, if drivers are caught speeding by the police or have a wreck, then they are punished by a ticket and your discipline program.

In this example, management has inconsistent enforcement. The time bonus (getting there sooner) is soon, certain, and positive. The enforcement (discipline for getting there late) is soon, certain, and negative. The bonus (driver awards based on on-time deliveries) is delayed, certain (if you speed), and positive. The discipline (a ticket and discipline) is delayed (may go to court to try to beat it), uncertain (maybe they won't catch me), and negative.

Now, which rewards and punishments will succeed? What type of attitude and morale will the drivers have? Soon, certain, positive rewards almost always have more influence on behavior than delayed, uncertain, and negative punishments. So most drivers will choose to speed. Also, you will find that the drivers who are caught speeding or who have accidents will have bad attitudes because they are being punished for the same behaviors that others are being rewarded for.

So what would you do to fix the system? Change the measurements and the rewards. Why? Because the rewards system is rewarding the wrong behavior by frequently providing soon, certain, positive rewards for breaking the rules and providing delayed, uncertain, and negative punishments when people have an incident.

In this example you could:

a. Perform a time and motion study to set reasonable targets for driving time, delivery time, and break times so that the work schedule is doable in the time scheduled.

b. Place a computer/video monitor on the vehicles to monitor the speed and driving performance. Reward those that consistently follow the speed limits, drive safely, and take appropriate breaks.

c. Provide a system for drivers to report problems experienced during deliveries so that they aren't punished for problems that they didn't create. Train the drivers to find the Root Causes of the problems so that they can report problems and recommend solutions based on the Root cause analysis. Finally, reward the drivers for using the system.

d. Drop the system that punishes for late deliveries and instead reward drivers for safe performance and reporting problems they experience making deliveries on time. Also, develop a system to reward people for implementing changes that effectively fix problems that are identified by drivers.

e. Drop automatic punishments for accidents and instead implement a program to investigate accidents and determine their Root Causes. Company punishments will only happen based on finding clear violations of well understood, well enforced laws and SPAC that were within the driver's control to follow.

f. Get driver review and recommendations to improve the recommendations above so that they think the corrective actions will be even more effective.

g. If possible, test the new program on a fraction of the fleet and measure the performance improvement before and after the corrective actions are implemented.

h. Communicate the new program to all involved. Explain how the old system failed and the results that were unacceptable. Explain the new system, how it was developed, the driver input, the results of the test, and the rewards and punishments that will result from the new system. Train the drivers in Root cause analysis. Test-implement the new program for a couple of months and suspend all punishments but provide all rewards. Have management and supervision regularly audit the new system (tapes and computer records) to monitor the program's effectiveness and to provide regular feedback to the drivers about their performance.

- For your enforcement problems you need to identify the current rewards used (positive and negative).

- Consider changing the system to provide soon, certain, positive rewards for the behaviors that you want to see.

- You also want to identify any rewards that are being provided for violating the SPAC and consider removing them.

- You should also consider how you can get the workers involved in self-assessment of their following of the SPAC and Root cause analysis of any problems they experience.

- You also want to review your discipline system to make sure that it is based on Root cause analysis and consider changing it so that it is only used when a clear violation of well understood, well enforced law/SPAC that is within the worker's control to follow is consciously violated.

- You should NOT punish workers for not following the SPAC if it was not clearly communicated and consistently, positively enforced.

- Once you have developed your corrective actions, communicate them to those who are affected. This includes the old enforcement of the SPAC, why it didn't work and the results it produced, the new SPAC, the behavior you want to see, how it will improve performance, how it will be rewarded; and if a worker still chooses not to follow it, how that inappropriate behavior will be punished.

- Consider taking this opportunity to reinforce the actions to be taken by the workers when they encounter a SPAC that they can't comply with or that they get rewarded for violating.

- Consider implementing an audit or assessment program to periodically check compliance with the new SPAC to make sure that the new SPAC is generally being used properly.

Exception to the Rule:

- If you find that the SPAC was not used and the person performing the work is an exception and violates a rule that is clearly understood and positively reinforced, then this is NOT an Enforcement NI Root Cause. Why? Because the SPAC is being properly enforced and complied with by most employees.

- However, if you have a properly enforced SPAC, then you should consider using your company's discipline system. Many companies have a "progressive" discipline system that starts with formal warnings and gradually escalates to firing the individual if they can't eventually comply with company policy. The system should be well documented and the reason for using it should be well understood.

- In this case the reason for using progressive discipline needs to be communicated. Workers need to understand that the discipline was not because of the incident, but rather it was because the individual consciously chose to violate a well documented, well understood, generally well followed and positively reinforced rule and that the punishment was intended to change the individual's behavior because that individual had not responded to the rewards that the rest of the work force responded to.

- If the individual has repeatedly been disciplined for failure to follow generally well followed rules and the individual is fired as a result of not following a rule that caused an incident, then the whole history of the poor performance and the specific progressive discipline taken needs to be well documented and communicated to the rest of the work force.

- You should make sure that human resources/labor relations and legal are consulted before official action or communication is initiated.

Ideas for Generic Problems:

- If enforcement of the SPAC is a generic problem, consider an assessment of the current management controls and enforcement policies to determine the Root Causes of the failure to follow them and correct the Root Causes. The start of this assessment should probably be a thorough audit of the Management System and enforcement policies and a Root cause analysis of the problems that are discovered.

- Once you have determined the reasons that people are not following SPAC, implement corrective action.

- Consider taking this opportunity to communicate to the rest of the work force the SPAC, the reasons for the SPAC and the problems that were caused when the SPAC were not followed. This will probably require training.

- Consider implementing an audit or assessment program to periodically check compliance with the SPAC that you judge most important and that were not followed in the past to make sure that the SPAC is generally being used properly.

References:

- For more information about soon-certain-positive rewards, read *Rewarding Employees* (Newsletter) by Bob Nelson. Available from Nelson Motivation, Inc. Call 800-575-5521 or see www.nelson-motivation.com or e-mail info@nelson-motivation.com.

- *1001 Ways to Reward Employees,* (2005) by Bob Nelson, published by Workman Publishing.

- To find out more about time and motion studies, consider reading: *Handbook of Industrial Engineering,* Chapter 4.4, (1982), edited by Gavriel Salvendy and published by John Wiley & Sons, New York.

- *Motion and Time Study*, 9th Edition (1992) by Ben W. Niebel and published by Irwin, Homewood, IL.

- *Motion and Time Study: Principles and Practices,* 5th Edition (1978) by Marvin Mundel and published by Prentice-Hall, Engelwood Cliffs, NJ.

- *Motion and Time Study: Design and Measurement of Work,* 7th Edition (1980) by Ralph Barnes and published by John Wiley & Sons, New York.

- *Improving Compliance With Safety Procedures - Reducing Industrial Violations,* (1995) by Steve Mason, Helen Rycraft, Becky Lawton, Peter Ackroyd, and Vicki Scotney. ISBN 0-7176-0970-7.

- For a description of how to use TapRooT® for proactive improvement and auditing, see the *TapRooT® Book,* (2008) Chapter 4.

- To get System Improvements' assistance developing or performing an audit of compliance with SPAC, call (865) 539-2139.

no way to implement:

Check: You have decided that the SPAC was not followed or followed incorrectly because a method of implementation was not provided for the SPAC or because no practical way of implementing the SPAC existed or because too much time and effort was required to comply with it given the level of staffing and the amount of work that was expected.

Ideas:

- Develop practical ways the worker can apply the SPAC. This may include more time to perform the work, check sheets, changes in equipment, making equipment and procedures more available, or changing the job.

- Consider changing the SPAC to make it more practical.

- Once you develop a way to implement the SPAC or change the SPAC to make it easier to implement (but just as effective), you need to communicate the changes to those involved in the work.

Ideas for Generic Problems:

- If ways to implement SPAC are Generic Causes, consider recommending a review of current SPAC and its implementation to identify and correct other SPAC that are not practical to implement. Also, look for the reason that these SPAC are being developed and applied without considering how they will be implemented.

Check: You have decided that the SPAC was not followed or followed incorrectly because no one was accountable, responsible, or answerable for a specific job or action that was required but not performed, or there was no means to determine who was accountable for this particular application of the SPAC, or the people involved believe that someone else was accountable or responsible for the SPAC.

Ideas:

- Accountability has to do with the ability of management and the people involved to clearly identify who is responsible and answerable for particular SPAC. Corrective actions for this Root Cause should not include actions to enforce usage of SPAC, but rather should be related to making the individual responsible more:
  - clearly identified,
  - aware of their responsibility, or
  - closely observed during the performance of the work.

  Therefore, you should consider changing the work practices and controls to make an individual more answerable for their actions. Examples include: a signature requirement for receiving a delivery; adding a signature box for completion of a procedure and retaining the completed procedures on file; adding individual initial boxes for each step of a procedure; adding a quality assurance review of the work by an independent auditor; direct supervisory observation of the work; or some type of automated checking of the work.

- Once you develop a way to improve the accountability, communicate the changes to those involved in the work and their supervision and management.

Ideas for Generic Problems:

- If accountability is a Generic Cause, consider recommending a review of current SPAC to identify and correct other SPAC that need to have the accountability improved.

- Also, look for the reason that these SPAC are being developed and applied without assigning the appropriate level of accountability.

- Again, any changes in accountability that are made as a result of this review need to be communicated to all affected workers, supervisors, and managers.

Management System (SPAC Not Used)

Oversight / Employee Relations	**Check:** You have decided that this incident could have been prevented by management involvement in an adequate self-evaluation program with timely corrective actions; or by management hearing about a problem that they would have solved by applying resources to implement adequate corrective actions; or by communicating their concerns for quality workmanship, their beliefs, safety emphasis, programmatic direction, etc.; or by creating an appropriate culture or work environment, including the proper examples and rewards for good performance; or by ensuring that there is an adequate external operating experience review program.

Ideas:

- Continue to investigate to find the exact reason why there was a problem with oversight or employee relations. Once you have identified the Root Cause, you can develop effective corrective action.

- If you can't identify the Root Cause, consider improving oversight to identify the core problems and their Root Causes. This could include a one-time audit of the process, procedure, or policy implementation.

Ideas for Generic Problems:

- If oversight/employee relations is a Generic Cause, then you should consider recommending a review of current oversight and employee relations practices to identify the Root Causes of their shortcomings. This could include benchmarking your practices against industry best practices or other successful divisions in your company.

infrequent audits & evaluations (a & e):

Check: You have decided that more frequent audits and evaluations should have been performed to detect the type of problem that caused this problem and that if these audits and evaluations would have been performed, then the problem would have been detected and corrected without incident.

Ideas:

- You should consider developing an audit or evaluation program to detect this type of problem. The audit program could include management audits, supervisory evaluations, and/or self-assessment (observations) by the workers.

- Whatever types of assessment(s) you choose, you need to ensure that the assessments are being performed consistently and that the problems identified are being corrected in a timely manner.

- Also, the results of assessments need to be communicated to management and trended.

- Once you develop an effective audit/assessment program, communicate the program to all those who are involved (those being audited, those who will perform the audit, and the managers who will review the results). This could include training for those being audited as to:
  - the reason for the audit,
  - the way the audit is to be performed,
  - the performance that is expected of the workers,
  - the reason that this performance is deemed necessary, and
  - how the results of the audit will be used.

It could also include training for the auditors on:
  - the reason for the audit,
  - the way the audit is to be performed,
  - the performance that is expected by those performing the job being audited,
  - the reason that this performance is deemed necessary,
  - how the auditors will document the audit,
  - any special steps to ensure consistency between auditors, and
  - how the results of the audit will be used.

Finally, the training for the managers reviewing the audit results could include:
  - the reason for the audit,
  - the way the audit is performed,
  - the performance that is expected by those performing the job being audited,
  - the reason that this performance is deemed necessary,
  - how the auditors will document the audit, and
  - management's role in using the results of the audit.

Ideas for Generic Problems:

- If infrequent audits and evaluations are Generic Causes, then you should consider recommending a review of the current audit system to find ways to improve them and increase the frequency of audits and assessments until they meet the needs of management.

References:

- For more information about using TapRooT® proactively, read Chapter 4 of the *TapRooT® Book,* (2008) or attend the 5-Day TapRooT® Team Leader Training. Call (865) 539-2139 for more information about course dates and locations.

Management System (Oversight/Employee Relations)

- You can also sponsor an on-site TapRooT® Auditing Class customized to your needs. Call System Improvements at (865) 539-2139 for more information.

- *Guidelines for Auditing Process Safety Management Systems,* (1993) published by the Center for Chemical Process Safety of the American Institute of Chemical Engineers, New York, NY.

- *Management Audits: The Assessment of Quality Management Systems,* 3rd Edition (1997) by Allan J. Sayle and distributed by ASQC - Quality Press, Milwaukee, WI.

a & e lack depth:

Check: You have decided that performing more thorough audits would have detected and corrected the system deficiencies before the problem occurred and that more in-depth audits should be performed.

Ideas:

- You should consider improving your audit system to increase the thoroughness of the audits so that they would detect this type of problem.

- Once you develop an effective audit/assessment program, communicate the program to everyone involved (those being audited, those who will perform the audit, and the managers who will review the results). This could include training for those being audited concerning:
  - the reason for the audit,
  - the way the audit will be performed,
  - the performance that is expected of the workers,
  - the reason this performance is deemed necessary, and
  - how the results of the audit will be used.

It could also include training for the auditors on:
  - the reason for the audit,
  - the way the audit will be performed,
  - the performance that is expected by the workers,
  - the reason this performance is deemed necessary,
  - how the auditors will document the audit,
  - any special steps to ensure consistency between auditors, and
  - how the results of the audit will be used.

Finally, the training for the managers reviewing the audit results could include:
  - the reason for the audit,
  - the way the audit is performed,
  - the performance that is expected of the workers,

Management System (Oversight/Employee Relations)

- the reason this performance is deemed necessary,
- how the auditors will document the audit, and
- management's role in using the results of the audit.

Ideas for Generic Problems:

- If the depth and thoroughness of audits are Generic Causes, consider recommending a review of the current audit system to improve it so that audits meet the needs of management, including sufficient thoroughness so that issues are detected before problems occur.

References:

- For more information about using TapRooT® proactively, read Chapter 4 of the *TapRooT® Book*, (2008) or attend the 5-Day TapRooT® Team Leader Training. Call (865) 539-2139 for more information about course dates and locations.

- You can also sponsor an on-site TapRooT® Auditing Class customized to your needs. Call System Improvements at (865) 539-2139 for more information.

- *Guidelines for Auditing Process Safety Management Systems*, (1993) published by the Center for Chemical Process Safety of the American Institute of Chemical Engineers, New York, NY.

- *Management Audits: The Assessment of Quality Management Systems*, 3rd Edition (1997) by Allan J. Sayle and distributed by ASQC - Quality Press, Milwaukee, WI.

a & e not independent:

Check: You have decided that more independent audits (performed by someone other than the owner of the system involved) would have detected the issue and caused it to be corrected before the problem occurred.

Ideas:

- Consider improving your audit system by recommending the appropriate level of independence of the auditors. This does not mean that all audits, or even a majority of the audits, be performed by independent auditors. A good audit program will have a balance of self-assessment, supervisory assessment, management reviews, and independent assessment. The breakdown of the different types of audits depends on the work being reviewed, the culture of the company, and the history of performance.

- Once you develop the right mix of self-assessment and independent audits, communicate the program to all those who are involved (those being audited, those who will perform the audits, and the managers who will review the results). This should include the reason that the independent audits are being performed and how the results of the audits will be used.

Ideas for Generic Problems:

- If the independence of auditors is a Generic Cause, consider recommending a review of the current audit system to improve it so the right mix of self-assessment, supervisory assessment, management reviews, and independent audits are performed so that issues are detected before problems occur.

References:

- If you would like System Improvements to provide you with an independent audit, call (865) 539-2139.

- For more information about using TapRooT® proactively, read Chapter 4 of the *TapRooT® Book,* (2008) or attend the 5-Day TapRooT® Team Leader Training. Call (865) 539-2139 for more information about course dates and locations.

- You can also sponsor an on-site TapRooT® Auditing Class customized to your needs. Call System Improvements at (865) 539-2139 for more information.

- *Guidelines for Auditing Process Safety Management Systems,* (1993) published by the Center for Chemical Process Safety of the American Institute of Chemical Engineers, New York, NY.

- *Management Audits: The Assessment of Quality Management Systems,* 3rd Edition (1997) by Allan J. Sayle and distributed by ASQC - Quality Press, Milwaukee, WI.

employee communications NI:

Check: You have decided that management has a belief in safe, quality workmanship, but one or more of the following causes needs to be corrected to stop this kind of problem.

    a. Management's employee communications program fails to communicate concerns for quality workmanship and safety.

    b. Management fails to provide proper examples and rewards for quality workmanship and good safety performance in the organization.

    c. Management's verbal / written communications and actions are inconsistent.

d. There is low morale or a feeling from personnel that "Management doesn't care what I do right. They only notice me to beat on me when I do wrong."

e. Employees take a short-cut (which causes a problem) because they don't have a "do it right the first time" attitude.

Each of the five issues above are often interrelated so that your corrective action plan may be complex and include multiple management improvement and communications improvement efforts. These types of problems are often found in conjunction with SPAC Not Used - enforcement NI. Root Causes and any corrective action that you recommend for the employee communication NI Root Cause should be coordinated with the enforcement NI corrective action.

Ideas:

- Consider developing a communication program that effectively and consistently communicates management's belief in safe, quality workmanship.

- Also, consider identifying inconsistencies so they can be corrected. Often these inconsistencies arise because of efforts to implement change (improvement).

- Because old habits are hard to break, the communication of the new vision needs careful development and continued emphasis. A good source for ideas to improve this communication and the entire change process is a book by John P. Kotter titled Leading Change, (1996) published by the Harvard Business School Press.

Ideas for Generic Problems:

- If the communication of the vision for performance is a Generic Cause, consider recommending a review of current improvement efforts and their communication so that the vision of performance and the communication of that vision are consistent and effective.

References:

- A good source for ideas to improve this communication and the entire change process is Leading Change, (1996) by John P. Kotter and published by Harvard Business School Press, Boston, MA.

employee feedback NI:

Check: You have decided that an issue that needs to be corrected was evident at a low level in the organization, but the issue did not get to a high enough level in the organization for the resources needed to implement corrective actions to be applied.

Ideas:

- You should consider improving the system that raises concerns and communicates them to the appropriate level of management.

- If there is no formal (or even informal), documented program to pass employee feedback to the right level of management, consider developing one. This could include:
  - developing a problem/issues reporting system,
  - developing a screening committee or system to evaluate and dispose concerns,
  - promoting, encouraging, and rewarding those who use the system, and
  - removing any impediments to using the system.

- If you develop improvements to your problem/issues reporting system, consider communicating the improvements, including the reasons for the improvements, to those who will use the system.

Ideas for Generic Problems:

- Finally, since this is a programmatic issue, it is probably a Generic Cause. Review whatever changes are proposed to see if there are other issues with the way problems are reported and communicated to management so that these could be solved at the same time.

 Check: You have decided that the problem was caused by failure to provide effective, timely corrective actions for known deficiencies (recurring failures).

Ideas:

- First, you should consider implementing effective, timely corrective actions for the uncorrected problem that caused you to select this Root Cause.

- Second, you need to consider ways to improve your corrective action system so that effective, timely corrective actions are implemented for identified problems.

- The types of corrective actions needed depend on the reasons for effective, timely corrective actions not being implemented. Therefore, you should consider continuing your investigation to the Root Causes of the corrective action failure.

Ideas for Generic Problems:

- If you find that failure to implement effective, timely corrective actions is a generic problem, then you should consider continuing your investigation to identify all the problems that are causing the corrective action system to fail and then implement effective improvements to the system.

corrective action NI:

Check: You have decided that the corrective action recommended in the past needs to be improved. (This may include a lack of corrective action for past incidents.)

Ideas:

- Recommend effective corrective actions! Before you can do this you need to understand the Root Causes of the problem. Therefore, you should continue to analyze the problem's Root Causes.

- Statistical Process Control (SPC) may help analyze the causes of repeat failures and develop corrective actions.

- If you cannot find the problem's Root Causes, consider conducting a Safeguards Analysis (Chapter 10 of the *TapRooT® Book,* 2008) to identify potential Safeguards that you could add to reduce the likelihood of recurrence.

- You may consider redesigning the equipment to eliminate the process or equipment that is causing the repeat failures.

- Also, keep a list of repeat failures that were attributed to the corrective actions needing improvement. This will improve the consistency of analysis of repeat failures.

- Also, consider ways to improve your corrective action system so that effective, timely corrective actions are implemented for identified problems. The types of corrective actions needed depend on the reasons the corrective action needs improvement.
  a. If no corrective action was recommended for a known problem, consider revising your problem reporting and root cause analysis procedures to include guidance on developing corrective actions for problems.
  b. Also, consider discussing with management and others involved the need for effective corrective actions and how the failure to develop corrective actions caused this problem.
  c. If the corrective action addressed only the symptoms of a problem and failed to address the previous deficiency's Root Causes, consider improving your root cause analysis system. This may require implementing a state-of-the-art root cause analysis system (TapRooT®) or improving the use of the system. Review the following to identify potential improvements:
     - your procedures for root cause analysis,
     - the initial training you provide,
     - specialized training for facilitators & human performance investigators,
     - continuing training to improve skills,

Management System (Corrective Action)

113

- your review of incident reports and corrective actions, and
- the field practices for performing root cause analysis.

d. Also, review the "SMARTER" concept (Chapter 3 of the TapRooT® Book, 2008) for ideas on how to improve corrective actions and make them more effective.

e. If an effective corrective action was initially proposed, but the corrective action that was implemented was not according to the initial corrective action recommended, find out why the changes were made and implement a corrective action to strengthen the corrective action process (perhaps by adding verification and validation steps to the process).

- Once you have identified corrective actions to improve your corrective action process, you should communicate these improvements to all involved.

Ideas for Generic Problems:

- If you find that ineffective corrective actions are a generic problem, consider conducting an audit of your root cause analysis and corrective action system. An independent audit would probably be a wise choice for this type of problem so that you could get information about how you compare to others in your industry or other industries.

References:

- For more information about System Improvements' independent audits of root cause analysis and corrective action systems, call (865) 539-2139, or see www.taproot.com.

- For more information about SPC, read: *Building Continual Improvement* by Donald J. Wheeler, (2001) published by SPC Press, Knoxville, TN, and *Understanding Statistical Process Control* by Donald J. Wheeler and David S. Chambers, published by SPC Press, Knoxville, TN.

- *Making Sense of Data,* (2003) by Donald J. Wheeler, published by SPC Press.

- *TapRooT® Book,* (2008) Chapter 3, Step 7.

corrective action not yet implemented:

Check: You have decided that the corrective action for a problem that was previously identified was not implemented soon enough.

Ideas:

- First, fix the specific cause of the repeat failure.

- Consider recommending action to expedite the implementation of the already existing corrective action.

- Consider recommending interim compensatory action that can be implemented immediately as a stop-gap measure (even though it may not be as effective as the more extensive corrective action). The goal of the interim compensatory action is to reduce the likelihood of the incident recurring or to mitigate the consequences of the incident if it does recur while you implement the longer term corrective action. If you cannot develop appropriate interim corrective action and if the consequences of another failure of this type are unacceptable, consider stopping production or shutting down the facility until the problem can be corrected.

- Also, consider ways to improve your corrective action system so that effective corrective actions are implemented in a timely manner. The types of corrective actions needed depend on the reasons the corrective action needs improvement.

  a. If the corrective action for a known deficiency is not implemented because management did not have the needed resources, consider recommending that in future budget and resource evaluations, a portion of the budget or manpower allocation be set aside to implementing corrective action in a timely manner.

  b. If the corrective action was not implemented because of problems in project design, abnormal length of the corrective action to implementation cycle, etc., then you should consider recommending a review of these processes with an eye toward a process redesign.

  c. If the failure to track the implementation of corrective actions leads to unacceptable delays in the implementation of corrective actions, you should consider recommending an accurate and effective corrective action tracking system be implemented.

  d. If a tracking system was in place but management puts no emphasis on implementing corrective actions, you should consider a management briefing to explain how the lack of emphasis impacted this incident and could impact future incidents.

  e. If other less important corrective actions were being implemented before this important corrective action, consider developing a system to evaluate and rank corrective actions and then schedule them using an integrated, resource-loaded schedule.

- Once you have identified corrective actions to improve your corrective action process, you should communicate these improvements to all involved.

Ideas for Generic Problems:

- If you find that ineffective corrective actions are a generic problem, consider conducting an audit of your corrective action system.

- An independent audit would probably be a wise choice for this type of problem so that you could get information about how you compare to others in your industry or other industries.

References:

- For more information about System Improvements' independent audits of corrective action systems, call (865) 539-2139.

- *TapRooT® Book,* (2008) Chapter 3, Step 7.

trending NI:

Check: You have decided that the trends from previous incidents or audits/ observations should have been used to identify the problem related to this Causal Factor/issue and that, by using these trends to discover the problem, effective corrective action that would have prevented this incident should have been developed and implemented.

Ideas:

- You should consider recommending improvements to the trending program to correct the problem(s) that allowed the trend to be missed.

Ideas for Generic Problems:

- If failure to detect problems using trends is a generic problem, consider the following improvements for your trending program:
  a. Start collecting your root cause analysis data in a database so that trending incidents, accidents, and audits/observations is possible using software.
  b. Choose a database and software that allows trending on the Root Cause level as well as other levels in the Root Cause Tree®.
  c. Divide your data into similar work types so that trends aren't masked by averaging.
  d. If your data is unreliable, consider improvements in your data analysis and collection system from the TapRooT® Book, (2008), Chapter 5, "How To Get Good Measurements" section.
  e. Use Pareto Charts to identify areas where your improvement efforts will yield the largest payback for the effort invested.
  f. Use Process Behavior Charts to detect trends in data over time.
  g. Use special Process Behavior Charts to detect trends in infrequently occurring data. Interval Process Behavior Charts should be used to detect improvements and Rate Process Behavior Charts should be used to spot problems.

References:

- *TapRooT® Book,* (2008) Chapter 5 by Mark Paradies and Linda Unger, published by System Improvements, Knoxville, TN. Call (865) 539-2139, see www.taproot.com, or e-mail info@taproot.com.

Management System (Corrective Action)

- For more information about SPC, read: *Building Continual Improvement* by Donald J. Wheeler, (2001) published by SPC Press, Knoxville, TN, and *Understanding Statistical Process Control* by Donald J. Wheeler and David S. Chambers, published by SPC Press, Knoxville, TN.

- *Making Sense of Data,* (2003) by Donald J. Wheeler, published by SPC Press.

- For training on improved trending, attend the 2-Day TapRooT® Advanced Trending Techniques Course. For information see www.taproot.com, or call (865) 539-2139, or e-mail info@taproot.com.

HUMAN ENGINEERING

Check: You have decided that a difficulty results from poor human-machine interface design (problems caused by poorly designed or inadequate relationship between a person and the equipment, facility, or system he/she works with), poor work environment, system complexity, or non-fault tolerant system problems where an error is not detectable or not recoverable.

Ideas:

- You should continue to analyze the cause of this problem to find the Root Cause(s) of the human engineering problem. You can then correct the Root Causes.

- If you can't identify the Root Causes, then perform a Safeguards Analysis (Chapter 10 of the *TapRooT® Book,* 2008) to identify potential Safeguards that you could add to reduce the likelihood of this problem recurring.

Ideas for Generic Problems:

- If you find that poor human engineering is a Generic Cause, then you should consider recommending a complete human performance review of your systems, procedures, and training. This may require hiring human factors experts to perform an on-site review.

- To develop improved human engineering, you should become familiar with applicable regulations, industry standards, company policies, and industry good practices that apply to the work being performed.

- Also, the best trade-off among human factors designs, procedures, and training is difficult to judge, but the three are certainly interrelated. Multiple, overlapping corrective actions that include human factors, training, and procedures may be better than a single, partially effective solution.

Human Engineering

References:

- For consulting help developing a complete human factors review, call System Improvements at (865) 539-2139.

For more information about human factors design reviews, consider reading:

- *Manprint, An Approach To Systems Integration,* (1990) edited by Harold Booher, published by Van Nostrand Reinhold, New York, NY.

- *Human Factors Engineering Review Model,* NUREG-0711 (2004) by the Nuclear Regulatory Commission and published by the Government Printing Office, Washington, DC.

- *Human-System Interface Design Review Guideline,* NUREG-0700 Revision 2 Volumes 1-4 (2002) by the Nuclear Regulatory Commission and published by the Government Printing Office, Washington, DC.

- *Human Factors Review of Power Plant Maintainability,* (1981) by J.L. Seminara and S.O. Parsons, published by the Electric Power Research Institute, Palo Alto, CA.

- *Handbook of Human Factors and Ergonomics,* Third edition (2006), by G Salvendy, 1760 pages, ISBN 0-471-44917-2. Published by John Wiley & Sons, New York.

- *Handbook of Human Factors and Ergonomics in Health Care and Patient Safety* (2007), by Pascale Carayon, published by Eribaum, Mahwah, NJ

Human - Machine Interface	**Check:** You have decided that a problem was caused by poor coordination or interaction of personnel with the equipment, systems, facilities, or instrumentation with which they work.

Ideas:

- You should continue to analyze the cause(s) of this problem to find the Root Cause of the human-machine interface problem. You can then correct the Root Cause(s). If you can't identify the Root Causes, then perform a Safeguards Analysis (Chapter 10 of the *TapRooT® Book*, 2008) to identify potential Safeguards that you could add to reduce the likelihood of this problem recurring.

Ideas for Generic Problems:

- If you find that poor human-machine interface is a Generic Cause, then you should consider recommending a complete human factors review of your system. This may require hiring human factors experts to perform an on-site review.

References:

- For consulting help developing a complete human factors review, call System Improvements at (865) 539-2139.

For more information about human factors design reviews, consider reading:

- *Manprint, An Approach To Systems Integration,* (1990) edited by Harold Booher, published by Van Nostrand Reinhold, New York, NY.

- *Human Factors Engineering Review Model,* NUREG-0711 (2004) by the Nuclear Regulatory Commission and published by the Government Printing Office, Washington, DC.

- *Human-System Interface Design Review Guideline,* NUREG-0700 Revision 2 Volumes 1-4 (2002) by the Nuclear Regulatory Commission and published by the Government Printing Office, Washington, DC.

- *Human Factors Review of Power Plant Maintainability,* (1981) by J.L. Seminara and S.O. Parsons, published by the Electric Power Research Institute, Palo Alto, CA.

- *Handbook of Human Factors and Ergonomics,* Third edition (2006) by G. Salvendy, 1760 pages, ISBN 0-471-44917-2. Published by John Wiley & Sons, New York.

- *Handbook of Human Factors and Ergonomics in Health Care and Patient Safety* (2007), by Pascale Carayon, published by Eribaum, Mahwah, NJ.

- *Medical Error and Patient Safety: Human Factors in Medicine,* (2007) by George and Barbara Peters, published by CRC.

- *Medical Device and Equipment Design: Usability Engineering and Ergonomics,* (1995) by Michael E. Wiklund, published by CRC.

labels NI:

Check: You have decided that a lack of labels or warning signs, or poor labels or signs, on components or equipment that must be located, identified, maintained, or operated to complete the task(s) led to the problem.

Ideas:

- You should consider recommending improved labeling.

- If no labels are on components, valves, equipment, gauges, displays, controls, or other items that need to be located, identified, operated, or maintained, you should consider recommending that they be clearly and permanently labeled.

- You need to be specific about the way that the items are labeled. To be effective, a label must be noticed, read, and understood. Often poor labels are either not noticed or are misunderstood. Therefore you should ensure that your labels are:

a. Easy to recognize, see, and read. That is:
- A color that stands out from the equipment background and that is easy to read. (Example: A white label with black printing on a dark blue piece of equipment.)
- Not obscured by other equipment or the procedure user's hand during operation or work.
- Uses an easy-to-read font using appropriate upper and lower case letters with characters that are large enough to see with less than perfect eyesight, in the worst lighting that a procedure-user is likely to encounter. In some cases, easily recognized symbols might be better than words. You should also consider language barriers if plant personnel speak a variety of languages. In this case, you may consider bilingual or multi-lingual labels.

b. Clear and unambiguous. That is:
- Near and obviously related to the item that it is labeling.
- Includes a well-understood name that is unique and is not just an acronym, abbreviation, or part/system number.
- Consistent with nomenclature used in the procedure. *NOTE:* If the procedures contain unclear or ambiguous equipment references, consider changing both the labeling and the procedure.
- In multi-unit plants, clearly and obviously distinguishes between the different units.
- For controls, indicates the discrete, functional control positions (on/off), and the direction to move for a desired control action (for example: increase/decrease).
- For displays, indicates the discrete item being displayed and the units of the display (for example: liters, mph, °C, or volts).
- For labels that mainly indicate location, sometimes a location schematic or overhead view as part of the sign or label can be extremely helpful.

- Check to see if you can find an industry or professional society standard that applies to your facility to help you develop a good practice for labeling.

- If you need to improve warning signs, you should consider reviewing the guidance in the 1997 version of the ANSI Labeling Standard Z535.4 and OSHA's hazardous materials communication labeling standard 1926.59.

Ideas for Generic Problems:

- If you find that labeling is a generic problem, then you should consider recommending changes to the design and construction of your facilities to ensure that new facilities are built with effective labeling

Human Engineering (Human-Machine Interface)

and that the labeling is checked before being turned over for normal operations.

- For existing facilities with a generic problem with labeling, you should consider recommending a plant-wide review for labeling problems that could lead to recommendations for new and corrected labels. This could lead to a plant-wide labeling improvement program.

- Finally, you should consider training the procedure users about the labeling problem (or problems) and the temporary compensatory actions that they can take to compensate for the poor labeling (for example, tracing the line to verify the valve's purpose).

- Also, you should train them on what they should expect for labeling and what they should do to report labeling problems that they find.

References:

For help developing labeling standards for your facility see:

- *Human-System Interface Design Review Guideline,* NUREG-0700 Revision 2 Volumes 1-4 (2002) by the Nuclear Regulatory Commission, published by the Government Printing Office, Washington, DC.

- OSHA's hazardous materials communication labeling standard: 29 CFR 1926.59.

- *Functional Naming Guide* available from System Improvements. Call (865) 539-2139 or e-mail info@taproot.com.

- ANSI Standard Z535.1 *Safety Color Code* (2006).

- ANSI Standard Z535.2 *Environmental and Facility Safety Signs* (2007).

- ANSI Standard Z535.3 *Criteria for Safety Symbols* (2007).

- ANSI Standard Z535.4 *Product Safety Signs and Labels* (2007).

- ANSI Standard Z535.5 *Accident Prevention Tags (for Temporary Hazards),* (2007).

- International Standards Organization (ISO) 3864 *Safety Colours and Safety Signs* (2006).

- *Human Factors Design Handbook* by W. E. Woodson, (1992). Published by McGraw-Hill, New York.

- *Human-System Interface Design Review Guideline,* NUREG-0700 Revision 2 Volume (2002) by the Nuclear Regulatory Commission, published by the Government Printing Office, Washington, DC.

For help with equipment and pipe labeling see:

- *Equipment and Piping Labeling,* DOE Order 5480.19 CH-2 (2001), Chapter XVIII.

- *Guide to Good Practices for Equipment and Piping Labeling,* DOE Standard DOE-STD-1044-93 (December 1998), U.S. Department of Energy.

- *Effective Plant Labeling and Coding,* (1989) Electric Power Research Institute, EPRI NP-6209.

- ASME A13.1 *Scheme for the Identification of Piping Systems* (2007).

Additional references:

- *Warnings and Risk Communication,* (1999) edited by M. Wogalter, D. DeJoy, and K. Laughery, published by Taylor and Francis. Hb: 0-7484-0266-7.

- *Handbook of Warnings,* (2006) edited by Michael Wogalter, published by Lawrence Erlbaum Associates, ISBN 0-8058-4724-3.

- Code of Federal Regulations (Pharmaceuticals) 21CFR211 Subpart G, *Packaging and Labeling Control.*

arrangement/placement:

Check: You have decided that the problem was a result of poor arrangement, placement, or situation of equipment or that the relationship between the display and its associated control was not obvious.

Ideas:

- You should consider recommending improvements to the arrangement and placement of the equipment. This could include:
  - lowering valves or meters so that they could be easily operated or read,
  - raising valves or meters so that people don't injure their backs due to bending,
  - moving frequently used equipment away from hazardous environments (don't require someone to lean across a hot pipe to turn on a light switch),
  - relocating a control so that it is near the indicator that is being controlled, or
  - guarding a switch so that equipment isn't accidentally actuated.

- Sometimes moving an item can be expensive or violate some system design criteria. The risk and cost of this problem should be considered to decide if the less expensive corrective action is OK or the more expensive corrective action should be required. If a less expensive corrective action is judged to be sufficient, consider:
  - Using easy-to-understand warning signs, labels, and painted areas to highlight the hazard,
        or
  - providing training to explain techniques that can be used to deal with the less-than-ideal arrangement/placement.

Human Engineering (Human-Machine Interface)

- Other items you may want to consider while making improvements to arrangement and placement are storage of documents, equipment, spares, flashlights, tools, etc. Improve the location of procedure storage and provide room for procedure usage during work.

- Also, you should consider training the workers about the arrangement/placement problem (or problems) and the temporary compensatory actions that they can take to compensate for the poor arrangement/placement (for example, getting a ladder and a helper to open a valve in an overhead pipe rack rather than crawling out on the pipe rack).

- Also, you should train workers on how to recognize arrangement/placement problems and what they should do to report arrangement/placement problems that they find.

Ideas for Generic Problems:

- If you find that arrangement/placement of equipment is a generic problem, you should consider a human factors/ergonomics review of the area to identify additional arrangement/placement problems that need to be corrected.

- In addition, you should consider training personnel to identify hazardous or error-causing arrangement/placement problems and the action they should take when they identify a problem. This action could include how to get problems corrected and temporary actions to take to avoid injury or errors.

References:

- ANSI/HFES 100-2007, *Human Factors Engineering of Computer Workstations,* (2007), published by The Human Factors Society.

- *KODAK's Ergonomic Design for People at Work,* (2004) by Eastman Kodak Company, published by John Wiley & Sons, Hoboken, NJ.

- *Handbook of Human Factors and Ergonomics,* Third edition (2006), by G. Salvendy, ISBN 0-471-44917-2, published by John Wiley & Sons, New York.

- *Industrial Ergonomics: A Practitioner's Guide,* (1985) by D. C. Alexander and B. M. Pulat, published by Industrial Engineering & Management Press, Atlanta, GA.

- *Handbook of Human Factors and Ergonomics in Health Care and Patient Safety,* (2007) by Pascale Carayon, published by Eribaum, Mahwah, NJ.

- *International Encyclopedia of Ergonomics and Human Factors,* Second edition (2006), edited by Waldemar Karwowski, 3 volume set. ISBN 978-0415304306.

- *Medical Error and Patient Safety: Human Factors in Medicine,* (2007) by George and Barbara Peters, published by CRC.

- *Medical Device and Equipment Design: Usability Engineering and Ergonomics,* (1995) by Michael E. Wiklund, published by CRC.
- For consulting help developing an ergonomics review call System Improvements at (865) 539-2139.

displays NI:

Check: You have decided that inadequate or unclear instrumentation, gauges, alarms, CRT (cathode ray tube), DCS (distributed control system) or other types of computer-based displays contributed to the problem.

Ideas:

- You should consider recommending ways to improve the display to eliminate the problem. Examples of ways to improve displays include:
  a. If essential information was not available, consider adding a display that includes all essential information.
  b. If a computer-based display system requires excessive paging back & forth between different screens, you should consider revising the pages to keep essential information on the same page or adding monitors so that multiple pages can be viewed simultaneously.
  c. If a display's face graduation & numbering fail to relate the readings in a practical way to the user's task, consider revising the display to use appropriate, easy-to-read graduations and numbers that are usable without conversion by the worker. To be easy-to-read and usable, the graduations should be consistent with degree of precision and accuracy needed, not require mental conversions. Use units that are meaningful to task, and include a scale spanning the range needed to measure the parameter. To learn more about developing useful displays, consider reading *Human Factors in Engineering and Design,* (1993) by M. S. Sanders and E. J. McCormick, published by McGraw-Hill, New York.
  d. If the worker is required to see something and his view is blocked, consider providing an unobstructed view by removing obstructions or providing other means to obtain a clear view (for example, a video camera).
  e. If there was a problem with an alarm, you should consider: adding an alarm for critical parameters that may need to have the worker's attention drawn to them; changing the alarm so that it gets the worker's attention, but is not so obnoxious so that it detracts from the worker's response; fixing the alarm so that the alarm does not produce frequent nuisance alarms; prioritizing the

Human Engineering (Human-Machine Interface)

alarms and providing smart alarm silencing so that the worker is not overwhelmed by multiple alarms that include unimportant minor alarms; or revising the alarm title or warning so that the message is concise, specific, and unambiguous.

f. If the display problem included problems with computer printouts, consider improving the printout to provide the information in a format that the worker can easily review so that it readily provides the information he/she needs. For example, a warning or out-of-spec condition could be printed in bold to make it stand out from other text.

g. If the display did not support the worker's mental model of the system, consider revising the display to present the information so that it reinforces the way that the worker thinks about the system. To learn more about cognitive engineering and mental models, consider reading *Engineering Psychology & Human Performance,* (1999) by C. D. Wickens, published by Harper-Collins, New York.

- Designing new displays should always include a human factors review, worker input, and formal test and evaluation before final implementation.

- You should also consider training the workers about the display changes that are being implemented and the reasons for the changes.

Ideas for Generic Problems:

- If you find that displays are causing generic problems, you should consider a human factors / ergonomics review to identify additional display problems that need to be corrected.

- In addition, you should consider training personnel to identify displays that need improvement and the action they should take when they identify a problem. This action could include how to get problems corrected and temporary actions to take to avoid injury or errors.

References:

For more information about designing good human factored displays, consider reading:

- *Human Factors in Engineering and Design,* (1993) by M. S. Sanders and E. J. McCormick, published by McGraw-Hill, New York.

- ANSI/HFES 100-2007, *Human Factors Engineering of Computer Workstations,* (2007) published by The Human Factors Society.

- *Designing the User Interface, Strategies for Effective Human Computer Interaction,* 4th Edition (2004) by Ben Shneiderman and Catherine Plaisant, published by Addison-Wesley, Boston, MA.

- *Human-System Interface Design Review Guideline,* NUREG-0700 Revision 2 Volumes 1-4 (2002) by the Nuclear Regulatory Commission,

Human Engineering (Human-Machine Interface)

published by the Government Printing Office, Washington, DC.

- *Handbook of Human Factors and Ergonomics,* Third edition (2006) by G. Salvendy, ISBN 0-471-44917-2, published by John Wiley & Sons, New York.

- *Human Factors Design Handbook,* (1992) by W. E. Woodson, published by McGraw-Hill, New York.

- *Human Engineering Guide to Equipment Design,* (1972) by R. G. Kinkade, published by Institute for Research, Washington.

- *Handbook of Human Factors and Ergonomics in Health Care and Patient Safety* (2007), by Pascale Carayon, published by Eribaum, Mahwah, NJ.

- *Engineering Psychology & Human Performance,* (1999) by C. D. Wickens, published by Harper-Collins, New York.

- *Human Factors Engineering Guidelines and Preferred Practices for the Design of Medical Devices,* (second edition), AAMI HE.

- *Medical Error and Patient Safety: Human Factors in Medicine,* (2007) by George and Barbara Peters, published by CRC.

- *Medical Device and Equipment Design: Usability Engineering and Ergonomics,* (1995) by Michael E. Wiklund, published by CRC.

- *Human Factors (HF); Human Factors Standards for Telecommunications Applications,* CENELEC ETR 039.

- *Human Factors (HF); Phone Based Interfaces (PBI) Human Factors Guidelines for the Design of Minimum Phone Based User Interface to Computer Services,* CENELEC ETR 096.

- *The Guide to Reducing Human Error in Process Operations,* (November 1991) Section A, SRDA-R2, by Dr. Les Ainsworth, Dr. Lisanne Bainbridge, Dr. Peter Ball, Ms. Mary Goode, Mr. Barry Kirwan, Dr. Andrew Shepherd, Dr. Ian Umbers, Mr. David Visick, Mr. David Whitfield, Mr. Jerry Williams.

- *Human Factors in Alarm Design,* (1994) edited by N. Stanton, published by Taylor and Francis. Hb: 0-7484-0109-1. Eb: 0-203-48171-2.

- *International Encyclopedia of Ergonomics and Human Factors,* (2000) edited by Waldemar Karwowski, 3 volume set, published by Taylor and Francis. 0-7484-0847-9. Eb: 0-203-18779-2.

- For consulting help developing a complete human factors review, call System Improvements at (865) 539-2139.

For more information about human factors design reviews, consider reading:

- *Manprint, An Approach To Systems Integration,* (1990) edited by Harold Booher, published by Van Nostrand Reinhold, New York, NY.

- *Human Factors Engineering Review Model,* NUREG-0711 (2004) by the Nuclear Regulatory Commission, published by the Government Printing Office, Washington, DC.

- *Human-System Interface Design Review Guideline,* NUREG-0700 Revision 1 Volumes 1-4 (2002) by the Nuclear Regulatory Commission, published by the Government Printing Office, Washington, DC.

- *Human Factors Review of Power Plant Maintainability,* (1981) by J.L. Seminara and S.O. Parsons, published by the Electric Power Research Institute, Palo Alto, CA.

- For consulting help developing a human factors review of your displays call System Improvements at (865) 539-2139.

controls NI:

Check: You have decided that inadequate equipment controls contributed to the problem.

Ideas:

- You should consider recommending ways to improve the control to eliminate the problem. A control should:
  - Have sufficient range of control.
  - Be easily adjustable to the required level of precision.
  - Be recognizable in terms of its function.
  - Be easily distinguishable from other similar controls with redundant coding (for example, labels, different colored and shaped handles, and different locations).
  - Be consistent with the expected mode of operation (conforms to the population stereotype and good human factors design). For example, if the mouse moves to the right, the cursor on your computer screen should move to the right.

- Two examples of ways to improve controls include:
  a. If similar controls are mistakenly confused, consider labeling the controls, color-coding the handles, modifying the handles or buttons so that they are different shapes, and moving the similar controls so that there is more distance between them.
  b. If controls were accidentally actuated, consider providing a protective cover.
  c. If the controls were complex, consider simplifying them. This could include making the controls conform to the worker's mental model and common population stereotypes (normal accepted practices). To learn more about population stereotypes, consider attending the 5-Day TapRooT® Advanced Root Cause Analysis Training (call (865) 539-2139). To learn more about cognitive engineering

Human Engineering (Human-Machine Interface)

and mental models, consider reading *Engineering Psychology & Human Performance,* (1999) by C. D. Wickens, published by Harper-Collins, New York.

d. You may also consider automating the control. Even if the control is automated, you will need to consider keeping the worker involved and aware of the computerized control actions.

e. If the control automation is a problem, you should consider ways to improve displays to keep the worker better informed of the actions taken by the automation and give clear, easy-to-understand reasons for these actions. You might also consider transferring control back to the worker during times of low work load to increase their involvement with the system, maintain their skill with manual control, and increase their situational awareness.

f. If the control causes musculoskeletal problems (hurt backs, carpal tunnel syndrome), consider redesigning or rearranging it so that it is properly aligned with the body and, thereby, reduces stresses. Also, consider redesigning the control to reduce repetitive motions and reduce the effort to activate the control. Also, consider isolating the control from vibration so that the vibration is not transmitted to the worker through the control. Also, consider providing the workers with additional work breaks and training them in the postures that will reduce stresses on their bodies. This could include proper lifting techniques and proper adjustments of equipment to reduce the odds of repetitive motion injuries. *NOTE:* One study has found that proper lifting training may not be effective in reducing injuries unless other measures are also introduced. To learn more about this study read "A Controlled Trial of an Educational Program to Prevent Low Back Injuries" in the *New England Journal of Medicine,* Volume 337 (5), (July 31, 1997) pages 322-328, by L. Daltroy, et al.

g. If protective clothing makes using the control difficult, consider redesigning the control so that it is easier to use when dressed in protective clothing.

*   Designing new controls should always include a human factors review, worker input, and formal test and evaluation before final implementation.

*   You should also consider training the workers about the control changes that are being implemented and the reasons for the changes.

Ideas for Generic Problems:

*   If you find that controls are causing generic problems, you should consider a human factors/ergonomics review to identify additional control problems that need to be corrected.

- In addition, you should consider training personnel to identify controls that need improvement and the action they should take when they identify a problem. This action could include how to get problems corrected and temporary actions to take to avoid injury or errors.

References:

- *Human Factors in Engineering and Design,* (1993) by M. S. Sanders and E. J. McCormick, published by McGraw-Hill, New York.

- *Human-System Interface Design Review Guideline,* NUREG-0700 Revision 2 Volumes 1-4 (2002) by the Nuclear Regulatory Commission, published by the Government Printing Office, Washington, DC.

- *Handbook of Human Factors and Ergonomics,* Third edition, (2006) by G. Salvendy, ISBN 0-471-44917-2, published by John Wiley & Sons, New York.

- *Handbook of Human Factors and Ergonomics in Health Care and Patient Safety* (2007), by Pascale Carayon, published by Eribaum, Mahwah, NJ.

- *Human Factors Design Handbook,* (1992) by W. E. Woodson, published by McGraw-Hill, New York.

- *Human Engineering Guide to Equipment Design,* (1972) by R. G. Kinkade, published by Institute for Research, Washington.

- *Engineering Psychology & Human Performance,* (1999) by C. D. Wickens, published by Harper-Collins, New York.

- *Human Factors Engineering Guidelines and Preferred Practices for the Design of Medical Devices,* (second edition), AAMI HE.

- *Medical Error and Patient Safety: Human Factors in Medicine,* (2007) by George and Barbara Peters, published by CRC.

- *Medical Device and Equipment Design: Usability Engineering and Ergonomics,* (1995) by Michael E. Wiklund, published by CRC.

- *Human Factors (HF); Guide for Usability Evaluations of Telecommunications Systems and Services,* CENELEC ETR 095.

- ANSI/HFES 100-2007, *Human Factors Engineering of Computer Workstations,* (2007) published by The Human Factors Society.

- *The Guide to Reducing Human Error in Process Operations* (November 1991) Section A, SRDA-R2, by Dr. Les Ainsworth, Dr. Lisanne Bainbridge, Dr. Peter Ball, Ms. Mary Goode, Mr. Barry Kirwan, Dr. Andrew Shepherd, Dr. Ian Umbers, Mr. David Visick, Mr. David Whitfield, Mr. Jerry Williams.

- *International Encyclopedia of Ergonomics and Human Factors,* (2000) edited by Waldemar Karwowski, 3 volume set, published by Taylor and Francis. 0-7484-0847-9. Eb: 0-203-18779-2.

Human Engineering (Human-Machine Interface)

- For consulting help developing a human factors review of your controls, call System Improvements at (865) 539-2139.

monitoring alertness NI:

Check: You have decided that the problem was related to loss of performance over time while monitoring. (The job was too boring.)

Ideas:

- You should consider recommending the following options: (Order does not indicate preference.)
    a. Provide an alarm to alert the worker and relieve the boredom of monitoring.
    b. Provide an automated monitoring and response system to replace human monitoring and response.

    NOTE: This will probably leave the worker in supervisory control. You will need to consider ways to keep the worker informed as to what the automation is doing and to clearly indicate why it is doing it. You should also consider ways to keep the workers involved in the process so that they maintain their situational awareness and maintain their manual control proficiency.

    c. Rotate the person monitoring more frequently. (Experiment to find out how long they can monitor reliably and then rotate people so that they only monitor for less than that time.)
    d. Redesign the job to provide other tasks that don't compete with the monitoring task to keep the person alert and involved. (For example, playing the radio while driving.) Do not provide tasks that compete for the same resource. (For example, reading a book while driving.)
    e. Provide false signals to keep the worker involved. However, you should also consider that people may ignore real signals if they become accustomed to receiving only false signals.
    f. Consult the workers to see if they have ideas that would make the task more interesting without conflicting with the monitoring requirements.

- Fatigue can also combine with monitoring alertness problems. Consider training supervisors to understand that fatigued personnel should not be assigned to tasks that require a high degree of monitoring alertness.

- Also, consider testing individuals for their alertness before assigning them to a monitoring task.

- Once changes have been approved, consider training the workers about the changes and their intended impact.

Human Engineering (Human-Machine Interface)

Ideas for Generic Problems:

* If monitoring alertness is a generic problem, consider recommending a review of the jobs to redesign them and add more active tasks.

References:

* *The Psychology of Vigilance,* (1981) by D. R. Davies and R. Parasuraman, published by Academic Press, New York, ISBN 978-0122061806.

* *Engineering Psychology & Human Performance,* (1999) by C. D. Wickens, published by Harper-Collins, New York.

* For consulting help to redesign the job, call System Improvements at (865) 539-2139.

plant/unit differences:

Check: You have decided that a problem was caused by differences in equipment, displays, or equipment controls between the different plants/units.

Ideas:

* You should consider recommending the following options:
    a. Revise the plants, equipment, or controls so that they are the same.
    b. Clearly and boldly label the different equipment so that the differences are highlighted. You can paint different units different colors and print the procedures for that unit on paper that is shaded to match or has a colored border that matches the unit's color. (This may not work, but it may be worth trying if the cost of revising the facility is too expensive.)
    c. Train the workers and mechanics on the differences in the equipment. This is the least likely option to work, but you may consider using it as an interim compensatory action while you are waiting for the labels to be installed or equipment to be modified.

* You should also consider training the workers about the changes that are being implemented and the reasons for the changes.

Ideas for Generic Problems:

* If plant/unit differences are generic problems, you should consider developing design standards to standardize the human-machine interface at your plants.

* Once you have chosen a standard, you can then perform an interface review and find non-standard equipment and get it replaced or labeled.

Human Engineering (Human-Machine Interface)

- In addition, you should consider training personnel to identify plant/ unit differences problems that need improvement and the action they should take when they identify a problem. This action could include how to get problems corrected and temporary actions to avoid injury or errors.

excessive lifting:

Check: You have decided that the work required excessive lifting.

Ideas:

- You should consider recommending one or more of the following ideas:
    a. Provide a mechanical lift, come-along, hoist, or other device to reduce or eliminate the excessive lifting. Caution: Training and qualification on rigging loads need to occur before the new lifting equipment is used. Otherwise, the new equipment may be misused and cause damage or injuries.
    b. Redesign the job to eliminate the need for the lifting, to reduce the weight to be lifted, to reduce the number of lifts, to provide more rest breaks, or to eliminate twisting during the lift.
    c. Develop a standard for lifting that sets maximum lifts and encourages proper lifting techniques.
    d. Train the workers to lift properly and to recognize excessive lifts. *NOTE:* One study has found that proper lifting training may not be effective in reducing injuries unless other measures are also introduced. To learn more about this study, read "A Controlled Trial of an Educational Program to Prevent Low Back Injuries" in the *New England Journal of Medicine,* Volume 337 (5) (July 31, 1997) pages 322-328, by L. Daltroy, et al.
    e. Provide additional workers so that a lift being performed by a single worker is now performed by two or more workers to make the lift safe.
    f. Consider the use of back supports. *NOTE:* Research results are mixed on the effectiveness of back supports in preventing injuries. This action may not improve performance. Some believe that the use of back supports may encourage people to attempt unsafe lifts that they wouldn't try without the support. Others believe that back supports improve lifting by supporting the back and reminding the worker to lift safely.
- Consider training the workers on any changes that are implemented and the reasons for the changes.

Human Engineering (Human-Machine Interface)

Ideas for Generic Problems:

- If excessive lifting is a generic problem, consider recommending a lifting review. The review should focus on the various lifts that are performed and recommend ideas to reduce the risk during lifting.

References:

- A good reference to decide if the lifting was excessive is the *NIOSH Lifting Guidelines* (Applications Manual for the Revised NIOSH Lifting Equation (PB94-176930LJM), US Department of Health & Human Services). Available at www.cdc.gov.

Software that automates the NIOSH Lifting Guidelines' calculations include:

- LIFTCALC (Joseph Townsend, SAFECO Insurance Companies, SAFECO Plaza, Seattle, WA 98185)

- Ergotrack (Heather Main, Performance Track Software, Inc., PO Box 787, Carrboro, NC 27510).

References that can be consulted to help you design workstations or work processes to reduce heavy lifting problems include:

- *KODAK's Ergonomic Design for People at Work,* (2004) by Eastman Kodak Company, published by John Wiley & Sons, Hoboken, NJ.

- *Industrial Ergonomics: A Practitioner's Guide,* (1985) by D. C. Alexander and B. M. Pulat, published by Industrial Engineering & Management Press, Atlanta, GA.

- *Ergonomic Design of Material Handling Systems,* (1997) by Karl H. E. Kroemer, published by CRC Press, LLC, Boca Raton, FL, ISBN 1-56670-224-0.

- *Handbook of Human Factors and Ergonomics in Health Care and Patient Safety* (2007), by Pascale Carayon, published by Eribaum, Mahwah, NJ.

- To learn more about a study that shows that proper lifting training may not improve the back injury rate, consider reading "A Controlled Trial of an Educational Program to Prevent Low Back Injuries" in the *New England Journal of Medicine,* Volume 337 (5) (July 31, 1997) pages 322-328, by L. Daltroy et al.

tools/instruments NI:

Check: You have decided that the problem was a poorly shaped tool that was uncomfortable to use, caused musculoskeletal problems, or required excessive force to operate; the tool transmitted excessive

Human Engineering (Human-Machine Interface)

vibration to the user; the shape or construction of the instrument caused the user to make mistakes or inaccurately perform the work; or the tool was the wrong tool to use for this work and the proper tool was available and would have prevented the problem.

Ideas:

- You should consider ways to improve the tool or instrument or make sure that the right tool is used.
    a. If the worker was using the wrong tool, you should consider training the worker on proper tool choice and making sure that the proper tools are readily available.
    b. If the tool/instrument design was causing the problem, you should consider recommending a properly designed tool that reduces the chance of injury or error. Improved tools, instruments, or workstations may be available commercially, or you may want to consult a professional ergonomist to help with the tool/instrument redesign.

Ideas for Generic Problems:

- If tool/instrument design or use is a generic problem, consider hiring (or contracting with) a professional ergonomist (preferably a Certified Professional Ergonomist or CPE) to review tool design and use.

- Once the proper tools have been identified and obtained, conduct training for the workers on proper tool choice and proper use of the tools.

References:

For more information about designing good human factored tools, consider reading:

- *Handbook of Human Factors and Ergonomics*, (1997) by G. Salvendy, published by John Wiley & Sons, New York.

- *Handbook of Human Factors and Ergonomics in Health Care and Patient Safety* (2007), by Pascale Carayon, published by Eribaum, Mahwah, NJ.

- *Human Engineering Guide to Equipment Design*, (1972) by R. G. Kinkade, published by Institute for Research, Washington.

- *KODAK's Ergonomic Design for People at Work*, (2004) by Eastman Kodak Company, published by John Wiley & Sons, Hoboken, NJ.

- *Human Factors Engineering Guidelines and Preferred Practices for the Design of Medical Devices*, (second edition), AAMI HE.

- *Medical Error and Patient Safety: Human Factors in Medicine*, (2007) by George and Barbara Peters, published by CRC.

Human Engineering (Human-Machine Interface)

- *Medical Device and Equipment Design: Usability Engineering and Ergonomics,* (1995) by Michael E. Wiklund, published by CRC.

For information on minimizing vibration read:

- *Vibration Solutions - Practical Ways to Reduce the Risk of Hand-Arm Vibration Injury,* HS(G)170, LSBN O 7176 0954 5 available from HSE Books, PO Box 1999, Sudbury, Suffolk, UK CO10 6FS, Phone: 01-787-881165.

- OSHA regulation 29 CFR 1910.241 - 1910.244, *Hand and Portable Powered Tools and Other Hand Held Equipment.*

For more information about diagnosing, treating, and preventing cumulative trauma disorders (CTDs) read:

- *Cumulative Trauma Disorders: Prevention, Evaluation, and Treatment,* (1997) edited by Michael Erdil & Bruce Dickerson, published by Van Nostrand Reinhold, New York.

- A good reference for machine guarding can be found at www.osha. gov/SLTC/etools/machineguarding/index.html.

- Australian Safety Standard AS 4024.1 -2006 Series - *Safety of Machinery,* www.saiglobal.com/shop/Script/Details.asp?DocN=AS929870415561.

Check: You have decided that the work environment contributed to poor human performance.

Ideas:

- You should continue to analyze the problem to find the exact cause of the work environment problem. You can then correct the Root Cause or causes.

- If you can't identify the Root Causes, then perform a Safeguards Analysis (Chapter 10 of the TapRooT® Book, 2008) to identify potential Safeguards that you could add to reduce the likelihood of this problem recurring.

- Since you have decided that the work environment is a problem, you could consider removing the person from the environment by automating the task or by providing equipment so that the task can be performed remotely.

References:

- *The Impact of Environmental Conditions On Human Performance: A Handbook of Environmental Exposures,* (1994) NUREG/CR-5680, Volumes 1 and 2, by D. Echeverria, V. Barnes, A. Bittner, N. Durbin, J. Fawcett-Long, C. Moore, A. Slavich, B. Terrill, C. Westra, D. Wieringa,

Human Engineering (Work Environment)

R. Wilson, D. Draper, D. Morisseau, and J. Persensky. Washington, DC: U.S. Nuclear Regulatory Commission.

- *Medical and Dental Space Planning: A Comprehensive Guide to Design, Equipment, and Clinical Procedures,* (2002) by Jain Malkin, published by Wiley.

- *The Control of Substances Hazardous to Health Regulations,* (2002) United Kingdom.

housekeeping NI:

Check: You have decided that poor housekeeping conditions contributed to the incident.

Ideas:

- You should consider removing the housekeeping hazard and developing a means to ensure that the housekeeping problem does not recur.

- The Occupational Safety & Health Administration makes the following suggestions:

"Passageways, storerooms, service rooms, and work areas should be kept clean, as dry as possible, orderly, and sanitary. Floors, workspaces, and passageways should be kept clear of protruding nails, splinters, holes, and loose boards. Aisles and passageways should be clear, obstruction free, and wide enough to account for traffic especially if mechanical handling equipment is to be used. Housekeeping and obstructions should not only be considered for every day activities, but also should be considered for emergencies and emergency egress."

Ideas for Generic Problems:

- If the housekeeping problem is a generic problem, you should consider developing a housekeeping improvement program.
  a. The program should be developed by those most directly affected by the poor housekeeping and should consider any regulatory requirements.
  b. One way to start the development of this program would be to benchmark your housekeeping with some other industry leaders with a reputation for good performance and good housekeeping.

- Once your housekeeping improvement program has been developed and tested, you should consider providing training for any worker, supervisor, or manager who is impacted by the program.

- You should also consider developing a housekeeping audit program to check the effectiveness of the housekeeping improvement program. These audits could be self-assessments, supervisory audits, and/or management audits.

Human Engineering (Work Environment)

References:

- For specific OSHA requirements concerning slips, trips, and falls, see the walking-working surfaces guidelines in OSHA Standard 1910.21.

- To review a statistical study correlating good housekeeping to reduced accident rates, see the article in *Professional Safety, Housekeeping & Injury Rate, A Correlation Study,* (December 1997) American Society of Safety Engineers.

- For even more ideas, read "Good Housekeeping Practices" in *Fire Protection Handbook,* (1986) edited by A.E. Cote by the National Fire Protection Association: Quincy, MA.

hot/cold:

Check: You have decided that excessive exposure of personnel to hot or cold environments contributed to poor human performance.

Ideas:

- You could consider modifying the environment with heaters or air conditioners to make the environment more conducive to good human performance. (The average optimum temperature for human performance is 68 to 70 degrees, although considerable variation should be allowed for the type of work and individual preferences.)

- You could also consider providing appropriate clothing to help the person deal with the extreme temperatures. This could include gloves and hats for cold conditions or cool suits for hot conditions.

- You could also recommend the proper intake of food and drink to help the person deal with the extreme conditions.

- In extreme cases (heat exhaustion and frostbite), you may want to limit exposure by limiting stay times in the extreme conditions.

- You should also consider developing training programs to ensure that all personnel working in the extreme environment understand the measures that they should take to avoid injury and improve their performance.

- Also, you could consider removing the person from the environment by automating the task or by providing equipment so that the task can be performed remotely. Automation or remote operation can lead to an additional new set of problems, so this corrective action should be analyzed carefully before it is implemented.

Ideas for Generic Problems:

- If the hot or cold conditions are a generic problem, you should consider performing a "work environment" audit. This would include measuring

Human Engineering (Work Environment)

environmental conditions at various work sites and proactively developing corrective actions for each problem that is identified.

- The implementation of these corrective actions could be prioritized by the history of problems that have occurred in the past and the importance of the work performed in each area that is analyzed. You should also consider asking those involved in the work to prioritize which corrective actions should be implemented first.

- Once this generic corrective action has been developed, it would probably be a good idea to consider developing training to explain why the measures are being taken and how the measures will impact the workers.

References:

- ASHRAE Standard 55, *Thermal Environmental Conditions for Human Occupancy*, (2004), published by the American Society of Heating, Refrigeration, and Air-Conditioning Engineers in Atlanta, GA.

- *Human Thermal Environments*, (2002) by K. C. Parsons, published by Taylor and Francis, London.

- *Thermal Comfort, Analyses and Applications in Environmental Engineering*, (1970) by P. O. Fanger, published by Danish Technical Press, Copenhagen.

- *Handbook of Human Factors and Ergonomics*, Third edition (2006) by G. Salvendy, ISBN 0-471-44917-2, published by John Wiley & Sons, New York.

- NIOSH Publication 86-113, *Criteria for a Recommended Standard: Occupational Exposure to Hot Environments*, (1986) by NIOSH, published by U.S. Government Printing Office, Washington.

- *The Guide to Reducing Human Error in Process Operations* (November 1991) Section C, SRDA-R2, by Dr. Les Ainsworth, Dr. Lisanne Bainbridge, Dr. Peter Ball, Ms. Mary Goode, Mr. Barry Kirwan, Dr. Andrew Shepherd, Dr. Ian Umbers, Mr. David Visick, Mr. David Whitfield, Mr. Jerry Williams.

- *Human Thermal Environments / The Effects of Hot, Moderate and Cold Environments on Human Health, Comfort and Performance* (2003) by Kenneth C. Parsons, published by Taylor and Francis, Hb: 0-415-23792-0, Pb: 0-4152-23793-9.

- *Standards for Thermal Comfort / Indoor Air Temperature Standards for the 21st Century* (1995) by F. Nicol, M. Humphreys, O. Sykes, and S. Roaf, published by Spon Press, Hb: 0-419-20420-2.

wet/slick:

Check: You have decided that adverse conditions that were the result of wet or slick surfaces contributed to the problem.

Human Engineering (Work Environment)

Ideas:

- You should consider ideas to reduce the problems caused by rain, snow, or other sources of wet/slick surfaces. (Order does not indicate preference.)
  a. You could consider enclosing or covering the area to provide an environment more conducive to good human performance.
  b. You could consider non-slip surfaces (for rain) or snow removal and ice melting chemicals to reduce the hazard of slipping.
  c. You could consider providing appropriate clothing to help the person deal with rain or snow. This could include cleats or special non-slip footwear.

- You could consider developing training programs to ensure that all personnel working in these environmental conditions understand the measures that they should take to avoid injury and improve their performance.

- You could consider removing the person from the environment by automating the task or by providing equipment so that the task can be performed remotely. Automation or remote operation can lead to an additional new set of problems, so this corrective action should be analyzed carefully before it is implemented.

Ideas for Generic Problems:

- If wet/slick surfaces are a generic problem, you should consider implementing the corrective actions that you have found to be effective in any area that could also provide the same hazard.

- Once this generic corrective action has been developed, you should consider developing training to explain why the measures are being taken and how the measures will impact the workers.

References:

- *Human Thermal Environments,* (1993) by K. C. Parsons, published by Taylor and Francis, London.

- *Handbook of Human Factors and Ergonomics,* Third edition (2006) by G. Salvendy, ISBN 0-471-44917-2, published by John Wiley & Sons, New York.

- *Understanding and Preventing Fall Accidents / An Ergonomics Approach,* (Nov. 2003) edited by Roger Haslam and David Stubbs, published by Taylor and Francis, Hb: 0-415-25636-4.

- *Measuring Slipperiness / Human Locomotion and Surface Factors,* (Dec. 2002) edited by Wen-Ruey Chang, Theodore K. Courtney, Raoul Gronqvist, and Mark Redfern, published by Taylor and Francis, Hb: 0-415-29828-8.

Human Engineering (Work Environment)

lights NI:

Check: You have decided that bad lighting conditions (too much, too little, or glare-producing) contributed to the problem.

Ideas:

- You should consider modifying the lighting to optimize human performance.

- This may include installing additional lighting, reducing glare, or (in rare cases) reducing light.

Ideas for Generic Problems:

- If lighting is a generic problem, you should consider performing a lighting audit. This would include measuring lighting conditions at various work sites and proactively developing corrective actions for each problem that is identified.

- The implementation of these corrective actions could be prioritized by the history of problems that have occurred in the past and the importance of the work performed in each area that is analyzed. You should also consider asking those involved in the work to prioritize which corrective actions should be implemented first.

- Once this generic corrective action has been developed, you should consider developing training to explain why the measures are being taken and how the measures will impact the workers.

References:

- *Lighting Handbook,* (2002) by Illuminating Engineering Society of North America (IESNA), published IESNA, New York.

- ANSI Standard A11.1-65 (R70) *Practice for Industrial Lighting*

- *CIBSE Code for Interior Lighting,* (1994) published by Chartered Institution of Building Services Engineers, London.

- *Handbook of Human Factors and Ergonomics,* Third edition, (2006) by G. Salvendy, ISBN 0-471-44917-2, published by John Wiley & Sons, New York.

- *The Guide to Reducing Human Error in Process Operations* (November 1991) Section C, SRDA-R2, by Dr. Les Ainsworth, Dr. Lisanne Bainbridge, Dr. Peter Ball, Ms. Mary Goode, Mr. Barry Kirwan, Dr. Andrew Shepherd, Dr. Ian Umbers, Mr. David Visick, Mr. David Whitfield, Mr. Jerry Williams.

- *Human Factors in Lighting,* (2003) by Peter R. Boyce, published by Taylor and Francis. Hb: 0-7484-0949-1, Pb: 0-7484-0950-5.

Human Engineering (Work Environment)

- *The Design of Lighting,* (1998) by Peter Tregenza and David Loe, published by Spon Press, Pb: 0-419-20440-7.
- Code of Federal Regulations (Pharmaceuticals) 21CFR211.44, *Lighting.*
- *Medical and Dental Space Planning: A Comprehensive Guide to Design, Equipment, and Clinical Procedures,* (2002) by Jain Malkin, published by Wiley.

noisy:

Check: You have decided that excessive noise caused diminished human performance and that this contributed to the problem.

Ideas:

- You should consider measures to significantly reduce the noise and vibration in the work area. This could include:
    - using vibration isolators on the machine or machines causing the noise,
    - installing baffles to absorb some of the noise,
    - enclosing the noise-producing source (sound proof box), or
    - using a sound-absorbing material to reduce the noise.

- New technology is also being developed to provide "active" noise control. This technology actually produces sound waves that cancel the noise source, resulting in lower noise levels.

- Also, consider the use of appropriate hearing protection. Remember what is lost when hearing protection is used. You may not hear alarms. You may find radio, telephone, or face-to-face communications difficult or impossible. And the loud noises that you are protecting against may mask smaller, but important sounds produced by different pieces of equipment.

- Once this corrective action has been developed, you should consider developing training to explain why the measures are being taken and how the measures will impact the workers.

Ideas for Generic Problems:

- If noise is a generic problem, you should consider performing a noise audit. This would include measuring noise at various work sites and proactively developing corrective actions for each problem that is identified.

- The implementation of these corrective actions could be prioritized by the history of problems that have occurred in the past and the importance of the work performed in each area that is analyzed. You should also consider asking those involved in the work to prioritize which corrective actions should be implemented first.

Human Engineering (Work Environment)

- Once this generic corrective action has been developed, you should consider developing training to explain why the measures are being taken and how the measures will impact the workers.

References:

- OSHA Standard 29 CFR 1910.95 G, *Occupational Noise Exposure.*
- *Industrial Noise Control,* (1993) by L. H. Bell and D. H. Bell, published by Marcel Dekker, New York.
- *Noise and Vibration Control Engineering: Principles and Applications,* (1991) published by John Wiley & Sons, New York.
- *Handbook of Noise Control,* (1979) by C. M. Harris, published by McGraw-Hill, New York.
- *Handbook of Industrial Noise Control,* (1976) by L. L. Faulkner, published by Industrial Press, New York.
- *Noise and Noise Control,* (1975) by M. J. Crocker, et al., published by CRC Press, Boca Raton, FL.
- *Handbook of Human Factors and Ergonomics,* Third edition, (2006) by G. Salvendy, ISBN 0-471-44917-2, published by John Wiley & Sons, New York.
- *Handbook of Industrial Engineering,* (1982) by G. Salvendy, published by John Wiley & Sons, New York.
- *Hearing Protection Devices,* (1997) by E. H. Berger and J. G. Casali in Chapter 81 of the Encyclopedia of Acoustics, published by John Wiley & Sons, New York.
- *Decisions and Stress,* (1971) by D. E. Broadbent, published by Academic Press, New York.
- *The Guide to Reducing Human Error in Process Operations,* (November 1991) Section C, SRDA-R2, by Dr. Les Ainsworth, Dr. Lisanne Bainbridge, Dr. Peter Ball, Ms. Mary Goode, Mr. Barry Kirwan, Dr. Andrew Shepherd, Dr. Ian Umbers, Mr. David Visick, Mr. David Whitfield, and Mr. Jerry Williams.

obstruction:

Check: You have decided that an obstruction that protruded into in a walkway or a normal workspace caused a person to trip or injure a body part by striking the obstruction.

Ideas:
- You should consider redesigning the work space to remove the obstruction.

Human Engineering (Work Environment)

- The Occupational Safety & Health Administration makes the following suggestions: "Aisles and passageways should be clear, obstruction free, and wide enough to account for traffic especially if mechanical handling equipment is to be used. ... Obstructions should not only be considered for every day activities, but also should be considered for emergencies and emergency egress." For specific OSHA requirements concerning slips, trips, and falls, see the walking-working surfaces guidelines in OSHA Standard 1910.21.

Ideas for Generic Problems:

- If obstructions are a generic problem, you should consider performing a work space audit to identify other obstructions and proactively develop corrective actions to remove them.

- Once this generic corrective action has been developed, it would probably be a good idea to consider developing training to explain why the measures are being taken and how the measures will reduce the likelihood of injuries.

References:

- *KODAK's Ergonomic Design for People at Work,* (2004) by Eastman Kodak Company, published by John Wiley & Sons, Hoboken, NJ.

- *Handbook of Human Factors and Ergonomics,* (2006) Third edition by G. Salvendy, ISBN 0-471-44917-2, published by John Wiley & Sons, New York.

- *Maintainability Engineering Handbook,* (1977) NAVAIR 01-1A-33, by Naval Air Systems Command, published by the Government Printing Office, Washington.

- *Human Engineering Design Criteria for Military Systems, Equipment, and Facilities* (MIL-STD-1472-D) (1989) by Department of Defense, published by Government Printing Office, Washington, DC.

- National Fire Code 101 Life Safety Code, by the National Fire Protection Association, Quincy, MA.

- *The Guide to Reducing Human Error in Process Operations* (November 1991) Section C, SRDA-R2, by Dr. Les Ainsworth, Dr. Lisanne Bainbridge, Dr. Peter Ball, Ms. Mary Goode, Mr. Barry Kirwan, Dr. Andrew Shepherd, Dr. Ian Umbers, Mr. David Visick, Mr. David Whitfield, and Mr. Jerry Williams.

- *Medical and Dental Space Planning: A Comprehensive Guide to Design, Equipment, and Clinical Procedures,* (2002) by Jain Malkin, published by Wiley.

Human Engineering (Work Environment)

Check: You have decided that poor coordination of human characteristics with the physical environment, facilities, or equipment contributed to causing a workspace that was too small for the worker to perform successfully.

Ideas:

• You should consider redesigning the work space to remove the hazard or increase the room available.

• Sometimes correcting a cramped quarters situation can be expensive or violate some system design criteria. The risk and cost of this problem should be considered to decide if the less expensive corrective action is OK or the more expensive corrective action should be required. If a less expensive corrective action is judged to be sufficient, consider:
   a. using easy-to-understand warning signs and painted areas to highlight the hazard.
   b. redesigning the work flow so that workers reduce their time and exposure to the cramped quarters hazard.

Ideas for Generic Problems:

• If cramped quarters is a generic problem, you should consider performing a work space audit to identify other problems and proactively develop corrective actions to improve performance.

• Once this generic corrective action has been developed, it would probably be a good idea to consider developing training to explain why the measures are being taken and how the measures will impact the workers.

References:

• *KODAK's Ergonomic Design for People at Work,* (2004) by Eastman Kodak Company, published by John Wiley & Sons, Hoboken, NJ.

• *Handbook of Human Factors and Ergonomics,* Third edition, (2006) by G. Salvendy, ISBN 0-471-44917-2, published by John Wiley & Sons, New York.

• *Maintainability Engineering Handbook,* (1977) NAVAIR 01-1A-33, by Naval Air Systems Command, 1977. Published by Government Printing Office, Washington.

• *Human Engineering Design Criteria for Military Systems, Equipment, and Facilities* (MIL-STD-1472-D) (1989) by Department of Defense, published by Government Printing Office, Washington, DC.

• National Fire Code 101 Life Safety Code, by the National Fire Protection Association, Quincy, MA.

Human Engineering (Work Environment)

- *The Guide to Reducing Human Error in Process Operations* (November 1991) Section C, SRDA-R2, by Dr. Les Ainsworth, Dr. Lisanne Bainbridge, Dr. Peter Ball, Ms. Mary Goode, Mr. Barry Kirwan, Dr. Andrew Shepherd, Dr. Ian Umbers, Mr. David Visick, Mr. David Whitfield, and Mr. Jerry Williams.

- *Medical and Dental Space Planning: A Comprehensive Guide to Design, Equipment, and Clinical Procedures,* (2002) by Jain Malkin, published by Wiley.

equipment guard NI:

Check: You have decided that unguarded equipment presented a general work environment hazard.

Ideas:

- Consider installing the necessary guards to reduce the hazard.

- You should consider conducting training for the employees concerning the hazard that was presented and the purpose of the guards. This training should emphasize that the equipment is never to be used when the guards are removed and that every time the guards are removed, appropriate lock-out/tag-out precautions should be used.

- If a required guard was removed, you should consider training for the workers about machine guarding and additional corrective actions under the Management Systems - Standards Policies and Administrative Controls NI section of the Root Cause Tree® (for standards that were not adequate) or the Management Systems - SPAC Not Used section of the Root Cause Tree® (for failure to use standards about machine guarding).

Ideas for Generic Problems:

- If inadequate machine guarding is a generic problem, then consider performing a workplace survey to identify all the inadequate guards and develop effective guarding where needed.

- If removal of required guards is a generic problem, consider the generic corrective actions under the Management Systems - Standards Policies and Administrative Controls NI section of the Root Cause Tree® (for standards that were not adequate) or the Management Systems - SPAC Not Used section of the Root Cause Tree® (for failure to use standards about machine guarding).

- Once the generic guarding problems have been verified and the corrective action is designed, consider providing training for the affected employees to teach them the purpose of the guards, what to

Human Engineering (Work Environment)

do if the guards must be removed (lock-out/tag-out), what to do if the guards are found to be missing or ineffective, and how to report other guarding problems that they may observe.

References:

OSHA standard, 29 CFR 1910.212(a)(1) says that:

"One or more methods of machine guarding shall be provided to protect the operator and other employees in the machine area from hazards such as those created by point-of-operations, ingoing nip-points, rotating parts, flying parts, flying chips and sparks. Examples of machine guarding are barrier guards, two-handed tripping devices, and electronic safety devices."

A good reference for machine guarding can be found at www.osha.gov/SLTC/etools/machineguarding/index.html.

high radiation/contamination:

Check: You have decided that high radiation or radioactive, toxic, or hazardous contamination contributed to causing an incident by making personnel hurry work to reduce exposure or by requiring protective clothing that diminished performance.

Ideas:

- You should consider recommending corrective actions that reduce the problems caused by high radiation or contamination.

- You may consider measures that would reduce the levels of radiation, toxins, or other hazardous contamination so that the worker would not be concerned and would not have to rush.

- You may also consider developing or purchasing improved protective clothing that is more comfortable or better suited for the work and, therefore, improves performance and/or causes the worker to rush less to perform the work.

- You may also consider removing the person from the environment by automating the task or by providing equipment so that the task can be performed remotely. Automation or remote operation can lead to an additional new set of problems, so this corrective action should be analyzed carefully before it is implemented.

- Once this generic corrective action has been developed, you should consider developing training to explain why the measures are being taken and how the measures will impact the workers.

Human Engineering (Work Environment)

Ideas for Generic Problems:

- If radiation/contamination is a generic problem, you should consider performing an environment audit.
  a. To start this audit, you would measure the radiation/contamination conditions at various work sites.
  b. You would also poll the workers to see where they believe protective clothing harms performance or places where they hurry to avoid exposure to radiation or contamination.
  c. You could then benchmark your contamination and protective clothing practices against other facilities with similar materials and contamination. The goal of this study would be to identify potential improvements to improve performance.

- Once you have completed you audit and benchmarking, you could then proactively develop corrective actions for each problem that is identified and implement improvements that you found in your benchmarking study.

- The implementation of these corrective actions could be prioritized by the history of problems that have occurred in the past and the importance of the work performed in each area that is analyzed. You should also consider asking those involved in the work to prioritize which corrective actions should be implemented first.

References:

- OSHA Standard 29 CFR 1910.97 *Non-Ionizing Radiation.*

- OSHA Standard 29 CFR 1910.132 to .138 Subpart I, *Personal Protective Equipment.*

- *Handbook of Human Factors and Ergonomics,* Third edition, (2006) by G. Salvendy, ISBN 0-471-44917-2, published by John Wiley & Sons, New York.

| Complex System | **Check:** You have decided that the problem was caused by the system being excessively complex or complicated. |

Ideas:

- You should consider continuing your investigation to identify the reason that the system was too complex and to find strategies for simplifying the system or the displays and controls.
- Automation could be considered as well as training and additional staffing. However, the problem may need a thorough human factors analysis by qualified human factors/ergonomics professionals before improvements that are effective can be identified.

Ideas for Generic Problems:

- If system complexity is a generic problem, consider performing a detailed human factors review of the system, displays, controls, staffing, and training to find strategies to improve system performance.

References:

For consulting help developing a complete human factors review, call System Improvements at (865) 539-2139.

For more information about human factors design reviews, consider reading:

- *Manprint, An Approach To Systems Integration,* (1990) edited by Harold Booher, published by Van Nostrand Reinhold, New York, NY.

- *Human Factors Engineering Review Model,* NUREG-0711 (2004) by the Nuclear Regulatory Commission, published by the Government Printing Office, Washington, DC.

- *Human-System Interface Design Review Guideline,* NUREG-0700 Revision 2 Volumes 1-4 (2002) by the Nuclear Regulatory Commission, published by the Government Printing Office, Washington, DC.

- *Human Factors Review of Power Plant Maintainability,* (1981) by J.L. Seminara and S.O. Parsons, published by the Electric Power Research Institute, Palo Alto, CA.

knowledge-based decision required:

Check: You have decided that the problem occurred because a situation or system was so complex that it required a knowledge-based decision for a successful outcome when a reasonable design could have eliminated the need for this high level knowledge and decision-making.

Ideas:

- To correct this problem you can consider several options. Each option will have different potential benefits, different implementation costs, and different probabilities of success depending on the exact nature of the problem. Therefore, this Root Cause is probably one of the best choices for getting professional human engineering help when developing corrective actions.

- You should consider these choices for potential corrective actions (presented in the typical order of preference - although your best choice may be any one or a combination of these actions):
    a. Redesigning the system or the human-machine interface to reduce the need for knowledge-based decisions.
    b. Providing procedures to change the knowledge-based decision into a rule-based decision and then training the person on the procedures.

Human Engineering (Complex System)

c. Providing additional training to make the knowledge-based decision a skill or rule-based decision.

d. Automating the response so that a human is not involved.

e. Providing artificial intelligence assistance to aid the worker with the knowledge-based decision.

- After selecting the changes, you should consider training the users on the changes and how they impact the job.

Ideas for Generic Problems:

- If knowledge-based decisions are a generic problem, you should consider a detailed human factors review by a human factors professional with experience in cognitive engineering.

References:

- For more information on decision-making models and knowledge-based decisions, refer to Jens Rassmussen's paper:
  - *On the Structure of Knowledge - a Morphology of Mental Models in a Man-Machine System Context,* (1979) RISO-M-2192, Riso National Laboratory, DK-4000, Rockilde, Denmark.

  or to his book:
  - *Information Processing and Human-Machine Interface, An Approach to Cognitive Engineering,* (1986) published by North-Holland, New York.

For more information about cognitive engineering, consider reading:

- *Engineering Psychology & Human Performance* by C. D. Wickens, (1999), published by Harper-Collins, New York.

For more information about human factors design reviews, consider reading:

- *Manprint, An Approach To Systems Integration,* (1990) edited by Harold Booher, published by Van Nostrand Reinhold, New York, NY.

- *Human Factors Engineering Review Model,* NUREG-0711 (2004) by the Nuclear Regulatory Commission, published by the Government Printing Office, Washington, DC.

- *Human-System Interface Design Review Guideline,* NUREG-0700 Revision 2 Volumes 1-4 (2002) by the Nuclear Regulatory Commission, published by the Government Printing Office, Washington, DC.

- *Human Factors Review of Power Plant Maintainability,* (1981) by J.L. Seminara and S.O. Parsons, published by the Electric Power Research Institute, Palo Alto, CA.

- For consulting help developing a complete human factors review, call System Improvements at (865) 539-2139.

Human Engineering (Complex System)

monitoring too many items:

Check: You have decided that the problem was caused by people having to directly monitor too many items or variables simultaneously, causing personnel to overlook or fail to notice necessary information.

Ideas:

- You should consider revising the human-machine interface to reduce the monitoring requirements or make the monitoring task more reliable. An example would be to integrate the variable into a single pattern display so that the person could simultaneously judge multiple variables.

- You may want to consider having a human factors professional perform a detailed human factors review to evaluate the tasks involved and the human-machine interface used in those tasks. They could then recommend improvements.

- After developing the changes, you should consider training the users on the changes in the system and displays and how they impact the job.

Ideas for Generic Problems:

If monitoring a large number of variables is a generic problem, you should consider having a human factors professional perform a detailed human factors review to evaluate the tasks involved and the human-machine interface and recommend improvements.

References:

To read more about the analysis of human factors problems, consider reading the following:

- *Human Factors in Engineering and Design,* (1993) by M.S. Sanders and E.J. McCormick, published by McGraw-Hill, New York.

- *Human Factors in Systems Engineering,* (1996) by Alphonse Chaponis, published by John Wiley & Sons, New York.

- *Human Factors in Simple and Complex Systems,* (1994) by R.W. Proctor and T. Van Zandt, published by Allyn and Bacon, Boston.

- *Human Engineering Guide to Equipment Design,* (1972) by H.P. Van Cott and R. G. Kinkade, published by U.S. Government Printing Office, Washington.

- *Engineering Psychology & Human Performance,* (1999) by C. D. Wickens, published by Harper-Collins, New York.

- *American National Standard for Human Engineering of Visual Display Terminal Workstations,* (1988) by American National Standards Institute, published by ANSI, Washington.

Human Engineering (Complex System)

For more information about human factors design reviews, consider reading:

- *Manprint, An Approach To Systems Integration,* (1990) edited by Harold Booher, published by Van Nostrand Reinhold, New York, NY.

- *Human Factors Engineering Review Model,* NUREG-0711 (2004) by the Nuclear Regulatory Commission, published by the Government Printing Office, Washington, DC.

- *Human-System Interface Design Review Guideline,* NUREG-0700 Revision 2 Volumes 1-4 (2002) by the Nuclear Regulatory Commission, published by the Government Printing Office, Washington, DC.

- *Human Factors Review of Power Plant Maintainability,* (1981) by J.L. Seminara and S.O. Parsons, published by the Electric Power Research Institute, Palo Alto, CA.

- For consulting help developing a complete human factors review, call System Improvements at (865) 539-2139.

Non-Fault Tolerant System	**Check:** You have decided that undetectable or unrecoverable errors contributed to the problem or the seriousness of the outcome.

Ideas:

- You should consider continuing your investigation to identify why the problem was undetectable or uncorrectable.

- You may consider having a qualified human factors/ergonomics professional perform a thorough human factors review of the system and tasks involved to better understand the information necessary and the controls needed.

Ideas for Generic Problems:

- If a non-fault-tolerant system is a generic problem, consider performing a detailed human factors review of the system, displays, controls, staffing, and training to find strategies to alter the system's fault tolerance.

References:

For consulting help developing a complete human factors review, call System Improvements at (865) 539-2139.

For more information about human factors design reviews, consider reading:

- *Manprint, An Approach To Systems Integration,* (1990) edited by Harold Booher, published by Van Nostrand Reinhold, New York, NY.

- *Human Factors Engineering Review Model,* NUREG-0711 (2004) by the Nuclear Regulatory Commission, published by the Government Printing Office, Washington, DC.

- *Human-System Interface Design Review Guideline,* NUREG-0700 Revision 2 Volumes 1-4 (2002) by the Nuclear Regulatory Commission, published by the Government Printing Office, Washington, DC.

- *Human Factors Review of Power Plant Maintainability,* (1981) by J.L. Seminara and S.O. Parsons, published by the Electric Power Research Institute, Palo Alto, CA.

errors not detectable:

Check: You have decided that errors being not detectable (by way of alarm or meter reading, etc.) during or after their occurrence contributed to the problem or its seriousness.

Ideas:

- You should consider adding an alarm or display to provide the person with the information they need.

- You may consider having a qualified human factors/ergonomics professional perform a thorough human factors review of the system and tasks involved to better understand the information needed.

- After developing the new or improved displays, you should consider training the users on the new displays and how they impact the job.

Ideas for Generic Problems:

- If being unable to detect errors is a generic problem, consider performing a detailed human factors review of the system, displays, controls, staffing, and training to find strategies to provide the information that the worker needs.

References:

For consulting help developing a complete human factors review, call System Improvements at (865) 539-2139.

For more information about human factors design reviews, consider reading:

- *Manprint, An Approach To Systems Integration,* (1990) edited by Harold Booher, published by Van Nostrand Reinhold, New York, NY.

- *Human Factors Engineering Review Model,* NUREG-0711 (2004) by the Nuclear Regulatory Commission, published by the Government Printing Office, Washington, DC.

- *Human-System Interface Design Review Guideline,* NUREG-0700 Revision 2 Volumes 1-4 (2002) by the Nuclear Regulatory Commission, published by the Government Printing Office, Washington, DC.

- *Human Factors Review of Power Plant Maintainability,* (1981) by J.L. Seminara and S.O. Parsons, published by the Electric Power Research Institute, Palo Alto, CA.

errors not recoverable:

Check: You have decided that errors being not recoverable before a failure occurred contributed to the problem or the seriousness of the outcome.

Ideas:

- Important, safety-related equipment should be designed so that detected errors can be recovered from before system failure occurs. Therefore, you should consider changing the system design or adding controls that help the worker respond once the problem has been detected.

- You may consider having a qualified human factors/ergonomics professional perform a thorough human factors review of the system and tasks involved.

- After developing the system changes, you should consider training the users on the changes in the system and how they impact the job.

Ideas for Generic Problems:

- If being unable to recover from errors is a generic problem, consider having a human factors qualified professional or team perform a detailed human factors review of the system, displays, controls, staffing, and training to find strategies to improve the system so that errors can be recovered from.

References:

For consulting help developing a complete human factors review, call System Improvements at (865) 539-2139.

For more information about human factors design reviews, consider reading:

- *Manprint, An Approach To Systems Integration,* (1990) edited by Harold Booher, published by Van Nostrand Reinhold, New York, NY.

- *Human Factors Engineering Review Model,* NUREG-0711 (2004) by the Nuclear Regulatory Commission, published by the Government Printing Office, Washington, DC.

- *Human-System Interface Design Review Guideline,* NUREG-0700 Revision 2 Volumes 1-4 (2002) by the Nuclear Regulatory Commission, published by the Government Printing Office, Washington, DC.

- *Human Factors Review of Power Plant Maintainability,* (1981) by J.L. Seminara and S.O. Parsons, published by the Electric Power Research Institute, Palo Alto, CA.

WORK DIRECTION   **Check:** You have decided the problem was caused or made more serious by a supervisory problem.

Ideas:

- You should consider continuing your investigation to identify the reason for the supervisory problem. If you can't identify the reason for the supervisory problem, you should consider performing a Safeguards Analysis (Chapter 10 of the TapRooT® Book, 2008), Change Analysis (Chapter 11 of the TapRooT® Book), or Critical Human Action Profile (Chapter 12 of the TapRooT® Book) to help you identify the problems.

Ideas for Generic Problems:

- If work direction is a generic problem, you should consider recommending a detailed review of your supervisory practices. The goal of this review would be to identify the causes of supervisory problems and to get successful practices implemented. One way to start this type of review is to review all your policies, procedures, and training that are currently used. You could then benchmark your practices against other companies with records of exceptional performance and good work direction practices.

 **Check:** You have decided the problem was caused by or made more serious by failure of supervision or work direction to prepare for a job.

Ideas:

- You should continue your investigation to identify the particular aspects of preparation that need improvement.

- Consider performing a Safeguards Analysis (Chapter 10 of the *TapRooT® Book,* 2008), Change Analysis (Chapter 11 of the *TapRooT® Book*), or Critical Human Action Profile (Chapter 12 of the *TapRooT® Book*) to help you identify the problems.

Ideas for Generic Problems:

- If preparation is a generic problem, you should consider recommending a detailed review of how supervisors/team leaders prepare for work. The goal of this review would be to identify the causes of preparation problems and to get successful practices implemented.
    - One way to start this type of review is to review all your policies, procedures, and practices that are currently required to prepare for work and the training that supervisors receive about work preparation. You could then benchmark your practices against other companies with records of exceptional performance.

References:

- *The Industrial Operator's Handbook: A Systematic Approach to Industrial Operations,* (2001) by H.C. Howlett, Pocatello, ID: Techstar.

- *The Industrial Operator's Handbook: Petroleum & Chemical Industries Edition,* (1996) by H. C. Howlett, published by Gulf Publishing Company.

- *PPE Made Easy: A Comprehensive Checklist Approach to Selecting and Using Personal Protective Equipment* (1990) by Jeffery Stull, published by Government Institutes, Inc. Available from ASSE. Call (847) 699-2929.

- *The Control of Substances Hazardous to Health Regulations,* (2002) United Kingdom.

- *Equipment Intended For Use In Potentially Explosive Atmospheres,* (May 2007), ATEX 94/9/EC, European Union.

no preparation:

Check: You have decided that supervision/team leaders did not provide preparation (instructions, job plan, walk-thru, etc.) for the work to be performed.

Ideas:

- Continue your investigation to decide the type of preparation that would have prevented this problem. Corrective actions may include:
    - pre-job briefings
    - tailgate meetings
    - job safety analysis
    - work packages
    - lock out / tag out
    - pre-job walk thrus
    - prepared checklists of personal protective equipment to wear
    - scheduling of sufficient time to perform the work
    - scheduling of people with adequate skills to perform the work

Ideas for Generic Problems:

- If preparation is a generic problem, consider developing guidance for supervisors/team leaders concerning the type of preparation they should perform.

- You could then provide work preparation training for your supervisors.

- Also, you should consider developing an audit program to check the effectiveness of your preparation guidance and training.

- Also, if you find that preparation is a generic problem and you have guidance and training for supervisors and field audits of preparation, then you should consider corrective action under the Management System portion of the tree.

work package/permit NI:

Check: You have decided that a better work package would have eliminated the problem or made it less serious.

Ideas:

- You should consider recommending corrective actions that fix the work package problem.
    a. If a standard work package was involved in this problem, consider correcting the items that you found deficient.
    b. If your work packages are developed uniquely for each job, consider developing standard work packages for jobs that are repeated frequently. These packages could be thoroughly reviewed so that problems could be avoided. Also, since supervisors would spend less time developing these packages, they would have more time to develop proper work packages for infrequently occurring work.
    c. If you have a large volume of work packages to be developed and your work packages are suffering because they are developed in a hurry with insufficient preparation, consider hiring professional work planners & schedulers to improve the quality of your work plans and reduce the workload on your supervisors.
    d. If your work packages are suffering because the people developing them don't know what should be in a complete work plan, consider developing training for the workers, planners, or supervisors who develop work packages. This planning should include emphasis on the particular aspects of work planning that are needed in your company or industry. These could include:
        - equipment identification
        - work methods
        - work sequence

- coordination between groups or teams
- safety precautions and warnings
- tailgate meetings
- procedures, policies, and standards to be used
- plant conditions to be met
- lock out/tag out requirements
- fire permits
- hot work requirements
- diving permits
- scaffolding permits
- fall protection
- personal protective equipment requirements
- applicable material safety data sheets
- doctors' instructions

- If the work package problem is related to an enforcement NI issue, you may want to read the enforcement NI corrective action guidance for more ideas to help you solve the problem.

Ideas for Generic Problems:

- If development of work packages is a generic problem and you have tried the ideas previously mentioned, consider implementing a formal work package review process to identify mistakes and add essential information before they are sent to the field to be performed.

References:

- *PPE Made Easy: A Comprehensive Checklist Approach to Selecting and Using Personal Protective Equipment,* (1998) by Jeffery Stull, published by Government Institutes, Inc. Available from ASSE. Call (847) 699-2929.

- *The Industrial Operator's Handbook: Petroleum & Chemical Industries Edition,* (1996) by H. C. Howlett, published by Gulf Publishing Company.

- *The Control of Substances Hazardous to Health Regulations,* (2002) United Kingdom.

- *Equipment Intended For Use In Potentially Explosive Atmospheres,* (May 2007), ATEX 94/9/EC, European Union.

pre-job briefing NI:

Check: You have decided that a better pre-job brief would have prevented or significantly reduced the seriousness of the problem.

Ideas:

- You should consider recommending action to prevent this kind of pre-job brief inadequacy in the future. This could include briefing the supervisor involved on the need for adequate pre-job briefs and the content that one would expect in an adequate pre-job brief.

- If this pre-job brief problem is related to an enforcement NI issue, you may want to read the enforcement NI corrective action guidance for more ideas to help you solve the problem.

Ideas for Generic Problems:

- If inadequate pre-job briefs are a generic problem, you should consider developing a policy that lists the content that you would expect in an adequate pre-job brief. What types of items should be included in a pre-job brief? The items depend on the type of work being performed, the risk involved, the potential for errors, the regulatory requirements, and any company or industry standards. Items to consider include:
  - information needed to perform the job
  - teamwork requirements
  - key work package requirements
  - important safety items like a review of the hazards involved
  - personal protective equipment and clothing requirements
  - lock out/tag out requirements
  - hot work or other special permits
  - expected outcomes
  - key things to communicate to the supervisor or plant workers
  - what to do if there is a problem or unexpected response
  - emergency procedures
  - emergency escape routes

- Many companies with excellent safety records require the supervisor to hold a "tailgate" or "tailboard" safety meeting before all significant work. During this meeting, the supervisor and the workers perform a pre-job safety review (or job safety analysis) to identify the hazards involved and the safety measures and personal protective equipment needed. The workers then know the hazards involved, the processes or equipment they will use to mitigate any hazards, and the actions to take if problems, unexpected events, or emergencies occur. The workers may suggest additional ideas to improve the safety of the job. You should consider recommending these types of pre-job briefs if you think they could be helpful and worthwhile in preventing future problems.

- Once you have developed a standard for what you would expect in a pre-job brief, you can train all affected supervisors and employees on the content of an adequate pre-job brief, including any requirements for pre-job evaluations and the tailgate meetings.

- You could also develop an audit program to check if the training was effective; if pre-job briefs are being performed and if they are adequate; and to develop recommendations to continually improve the pre-job analysis and the tailgate meetings.

References:

- *PPE Made Easy: A Comprehensive Checklist Approach to Selecting and Using Personal Protective Equipment,* (1998) by Jeffery Stull, published by Government Institutes, Inc. Available from ASSE. Call (847) 699-2929.

- *The Industrial Operator's Handbook: Petroleum & Chemical Industries Edition,* (1996) by H. C. Howlett, published by Gulf Publishing Company.

- *The Control of Substances Hazardous to Health Regulations,* (2002) United Kingdom.

- *Equipment Intended For Use In Potentially Explosive Atmospheres,* (May 2007), ATEX 94/9/EC, European Union.

walk-thru NI:

Check: You have decided that the supervisor should have walked the workers thru the steps required to perform an infrequently occurring and complex task and/or high-risk task and that a walk-thru would have prevented or significantly reduced the seriousness of the problem.

Ideas:

- If your facility does not perform walk-thrus, you should consider recommending that walk-thrus be conducted for this type of infrequently occurring or high-risk work.

- You would need to develop guidance for the types of work requiring walk-thrus and the items to be shown and discussed during a walk-thru.

- Once this guidance has been developed, you will need to conduct training for supervisors or work team leaders to train them to perform adequate walk-thrus.

- Finally, you could develop an audit program to check to see if walk-thrus are being performed and to provide feedback of the adequacy of the walk-thrus and the walk-thru training.

- If you have some repetitive jobs that involve high-risk tasks, you may want to consider developing a standard pre-job brief / walk-thru package that includes all the information needed and a lesson plan for conducting the walk-thru.

- If this walk-thru problem is related to an enforcement NI issue, you may want to read the enforcement NI corrective action guidance for more ideas to help you solve the problem.

Ideas for Generic Problems:

- If you have already performed all the items above and you still have generic problems with walk-thrus, you should consider performing a detailed review of the work being performed and the walk-thrus that are being performed.

- Then you should benchmark your work preparation activities against others with an excellent record for quality workmanship and safety in your industry to identify the differences in your program and theirs. This should provide you with ideas to improve your program and reduce the preparation problems. After you have tested these ideas, you will want to conduct training for all affected personnel.

References:

- *Job Analysis at the Speed of Reality,* (1999) by Darin Hartley, published by HRD Press.

scheduling NI:

Check: You have decided that the problem was related to scheduling the task.

Ideas:

- You should consider actions that will improve the scheduling and eliminate the problem.

- If you find that the employee made a mistake while rushing (because of excessive workload) to perform a task, you should consider reducing the workload or increasing the people available to make the workload more reasonable.

- If you find that workers are fatigued during the work due to the schedule or pace of the work, you should consider increasing work breaks or adding people to reduce the fatigue.

- If the shift schedule causes "normal" fatigue for workers, you should consider optimizing your shift schedule to improve performance. For more information about optimizing shift scheduling, see *The Twenty Four Hour Society,* (1993) by Dr. Martin Moore-Ede, published by Addison-Wesley Publishing Company, Reading, MA.

- If the task involved was not compatible with existing plant conditions, consider developing guidance for work planners or supervisors concerning the plant conditions required to perform this kind of work. This guidance can be added to procedures or become a part of computerized maintenance scheduling packages.

- If required periodic testing or surveillance was not performed because the supervisors or maintenance schedulers did not schedule it, consider scheduling and tracking aids that will help the person responsible identify what maintenance is required and what maintenance has been performed so that the appropriate maintenance to be performed is clear.

Ideas for Generic Problems:

- If scheduling work is a generic problem, consider performing a time and motion survey to analyze the work being performed and the proper number of people required to perform the task.

- Then consider developing schedule requirements to include in the procedures or the computerized work scheduling program.

- Next, consider auditing the application of the schedules to measure actual work being performed and to see if additional tasks are being performed that weren't included in the time and motion study.

- Finally, consider developing training for the supervisors and workers about the scheduling of work, problems that can result if work is improperly scheduled or if too much work is scheduled, and what they can do if they feel overwhelmed or rushed.

References:

For information about the latest sleep, fatigue, and shiftwork research, try these web sites:

- Circadian Technologies, Inc.: www.shiftwork.com

- University of Illinois Clockworks: www.life.uiuc.edu

- Society for Light Treatment & Biological Rhythms: www.psychiatry.ubc.ca

- Society for Research on Biological Rhythms: www.srbr.org

- Center for Biological Timing: www.cbt.virginia.edu

- National Science Foundation: www.nsf.org

- American Medical Association: www.ama-assn.org

For more information about fatigue, consider reading:

- *Making Shiftwork Tolerable,* (1992) by T. H. Monk and S. Folkard, published by Taylor and Francis, Pb: 0-85066-822-0.

- *Human Performance in Planning and Scheduling,* (2001) edited by Bart MacCarthy and John Wilson, published by Taylor and Francis, Hb: 0-7484-0929-7.

- *The Guide to Reducing Human Error in Process Operations* (November 1991) Section E2, SRDA-R2, by Dr. Les Ainsworth, Dr. Lisanne Bainbridge, Dr. Peter Ball, Ms. Mary Goode, Mr. Barry Kirwan, Dr. Andrew Shepherd, Dr. Ian Umbers, Mr. David Visick, Mr. David Whitfield, and Mr. Jerry Williams.

- SAE Transaction 113, (2004), *The Fatigue Avoidance Scheduling Tool: Modeling to minimize the effects of fatigue on cognitive performance,* by S.R. Hursh, T.J. Balkin, and D.R. Eddy.

To find out more about time & motion studies, consider reading:

- *Manprint, An Approach To Systems Integration,* (1990) Chapter 9, Workload Assessment & Prediction (pages 257 - 296) edited by Harold Booher, published by Van Nostrand Reinhold, New York, NY.

- *Handbook of Industrial Engineering,* Chapter 4.4 (1982), edited by Gavriel Salvendy, published by John Wiley & Sons, New York.

- *Motion and Time Studies,* 6th Edition (1976) by Ben W. Niebel, published by Irwin, Homewood, IL.

- *Motion and Time Study: Principles and Practices,* 5th Edition (1978) by Marvin Mundel, published by Prentice-Hall, Engelwood Cliffs, NJ.

- *Motion and Time Study:Design and Measurement of Work,* 7th Edition (1980) by Ralph Barnes, published by John Wiley & Sons, New York.

lock out/tag out NI:

Check: You have decided that the problem was related to an inadequate lock out or tag out of equipment that should not have been operated or worked on.

Ideas:

- You should consider discussing the problem you have identified and the way it could be corrected with the people and the supervisor involved.

- If your lock out/tag out requirements were not good enough, consider revising them. See the references below for more information.

- Once you have improved your standard, you would then need to train people about the changes in your standard.

- If people did not understand how to perform a proper lock out/tag out, you should consider training them about your standard.

- If people failed to perform a lock out/tag out, you should consider the instructions from the supervisor and the supervisor's involvement and support in the lock out/tag out process.

- If this lock out / tag out problem is related to an enforcement NI issue, you may want to read the enforcement NI corrective action guidance for more ideas to help you solve the problem.

Ideas for Generic Problems:

- If you have generic problems with lock out/tag out, you should consider improving your lock out / tag out system.
  a. One idea to start the process is reviewing the OSHA Standard 1910 and then performing benchmarking of your system with other companies in your industry with a reputation and record of safe work.
  b. You then could conduct a series of audits to identify all the major problems with the way your employees perform lock out/tag out and then develop comprehensive recommendations to improve your system.
  c. Once these recommendations have been tested, you would want to conduct training for all people involved and start a regular audit program to check that the recommendations are being implemented, to identify continuing ideas for improvement, and to compliment people who are implementing the lock out/tag out system properly.

- If the generic lock out / tag out problem is related to an enforcement NI issue, you may want to read the Enforcement NI corrective action guidance for more ideas to help you solve the problem.

References:

- OSHA Standard 29 CFR 1910.147 t. This standard is available on-line at www.osha-slc.gov/dts/osta/lototraining/std/147-ht-rel.htm. Training for this standard is available on-line at www.osha-slc.gov/dts/osta/lototraining/index.htm.

- DOE-STD-1030-96, *Guide to Good Practices for Lockouts and Tagouts*, (May 1996).

- OSHA Fact Sheet 89-32, *Control of Hazardous Energy Sources (Lockout/Tagout)*, (June 13, 1989).

- *Lockout/Tagout: A Practical Approach*, (2001) by Stephen M. Kelly, CHMM, CSP. This publication is a basic handbook for achieving compliance with OSHA's Lockout/Tagout standard and implementing a comprehensive energy control program. It contains many case studies to present effective techniques for ensuring 100 percent protection of personnel during service and maintenance of machines, equipment, and processes. It is available for purchase at www.asse.org.

- ANSI/ASSE Z244.1, *Control of Hazardous Energy - Lockout/Tagout and Alternative Methods.* Available for purchase by calling (847) 699-2929 or at the ASSE web site http://www.asse.org/shoponline/index.htm.

fall protection NI:

Check: You have decided that the supervisor, team leader, or person in charge should have ensured the use of proper fall protection equipment and that failure to use proper fall protection equipment contributed to the problem.

Ideas:

- If the reason for not ensuring the use of fall protection equipment was a lack of knowledge of fall protection equipment requirements and usage, consider conducting training for supervisors and employees. This training should meet the requirements of the applicable government, industry, and company standards. See the reference below for OSHA standards. You should also consider corrective actions for the lack of training under the Training Basic Cause Category of the Root Cause Tree®.

- If the reason for not ensuring the use of fall protection equipment was a lack of standards or failure to use existing standards, consider the corrective actions under the Management System Basic Cause Category.

Ideas for Generic Problems:

- If failure to use fall protection is a generic problem at your facility/company and your facility/company has workers that have potential to fall and be injured if they fail to wear proper fall protection equipment, you should consider stopping all work involving the risk of falling until proper fall protection standards and program are developed and applied, proper fall protection training is provided to workers and supervisors, and proper fall protection equipment is available for the workers.

- You should consider developing a fall protection audit program to ensure the proper use of fall protection equipment.

References:

- For a sample fall protection plan for the construction industry, see the OSHA Sample Fall Protection Plan - Non-Mandatory Guidelines for Complying with 1926.502(k) - 1926 Subpart M App E at: www.osha-slc.gov/OshStd_data/1926_SUBPART_M_APP_E.html

- *Introduction to Fall Protection,* Third edition, (2001) by J. Nigel Ellis, PH.D., P.E., CSP, ASSE Hard cover, available at www.asse.org.

- www.osha-slc.gov/SLTC/fallprotection/compliance.html.

You will find the following list of fall protection references:

OSHA STANDARDS

General Industry

- 1910.23, Guarding floor and wall openings and holes.
- 1910.66, Powered platforms for building maintenance.
- App A, Guidelines (Advisory).
- App C, Personal Fall Arrest System (Section I - Mandatory; Sections II and III -Non-Mandatory).
- 1910.132, General Requirements (Personal Protective Equipment).
- 1910.269, Electric Power Generation, Transmission, and Distribution. References 1926 Subpart M and contains additional requirements for fall protection.

Construction

- 1926 Subpart M, Fall Protection (Table of Contents). Includes standards 1926.500 to 1926.503, with Appendices A-E.
- Fall Protection - Construction (Subpart M). Lab Safety Supply EZ Facts (July 1, 1996). A general summary and discussion of the fall protection regulations.
- 1926 Subpart L, Scaffolds (Table of Contents). Several standards in this subpart contain requirements for fall protection. The following sections deserve special attention:
- 1926.451, General requirements (scaffolding).
- 1926.452, Additional requirements applicable to specific types of scaffolds. Addresses requirements for guardrails when used as a means for fall protection.
- 1926.454, Training requirements (scaffolds). App B, Criteria for Determining the Feasibility of Providing Safe Access and Fall Protection for Scaffold Erectors and Dismantlers, and App D, List of Training Topics for Scaffold Erectors and Dismantlers.
- 1926.104, Safety belts, lifelines, and lanyards.
- 1926.105, Safety nets.
- 1926.651, Specific Excavation Requirements.
- 1926.753, Safety Nets (Steel Erection). This standard is being stayed until the fall protection requirements for steel erection is issued.

- 1926.800, Underground Construction. Mentions fall protection (guardrails) required for jumbo decks.

- 1926.1051, General requirements (stairways and ladders).

- 1926.1060, Training requirements (stairways and ladders).

Shipyard Employment

- 1915.159, Personal fall arrest systems (PFAS).

- 1915 Subpart I App B, General Testing Conditions and Additional Guidelines for Personal Fall Protection Systems (Non-mandatory).

- 1915.160, Positioning device systems.

Longshoring

- 1918.85, Containerized cargo operations. Includes requirements for fall protection.

Preambles to OSHA Standards

- Fall Protection in the Construction Industry (August 9, 1994).

OSHA Directives

- Interim Fall Protection Compliance Guidelines for Residential Construction. STD 3.1 (December 8, 1995).

- Change to the Construction Standard Alleged Violation Elements (SAVES) Manual. CPL 2.34 CH-5 (August 6, 1990), 41 pages. Includes SAVES related to fall protection.

- Changes to the Construction Standard Alleged Violation Elements (SAVES) Manual. CPL 2.34 CH-6 (July 15, 1991), 35 pages. Includes some SAVES for fall protection related to ladders.

- Change to the Construction Standard Alleged Violation Elements (SAVES) Manual. CPL 2.34 CH-8 (August 3, 1992), 43 pages. Includes SAVES related to fall protection-related from 1926.800.

- Inspection Procedures for Enforcing Subpart L, Scaffolds Used in Construction – 29 CFR 1926.450-454. CPL 2-1.23 (January 7, 1997), 17 pages. Fall protection is included.

- Focused Inspection Program for Intermodal Container Top Fall Protection. CPL 2-1.27 (May 12, 1998), 7 pages. Provides guidance for enforcing 1918.85.

Review Commission Decisions

There are several Review Commission Decisions related to fall protection. Search results are located here.

- Standard Interpretations and Compliance Letters
- Standard Interpretations and Compliance Letters related to 1926 Subpart M, Fall Protection:
- 1926.500
- 1926.501
- 1926.502
- 1926.503
- Authority for 1926 Subpart M

ANSI/ASSE Z359 Fall Protection Code

- ANSI/ASSE Z359.0-2007, Definitions and Nomenclature.
- ANSI/ASSE Z359.1-2007, Safety Requirements for Personal Fall Arrest Systems.
- ANSI/ASSE Z359.2-2007, Minimum Requirements for a Comprehensive Managed Fall Protection Program.
- ANSI/ASSE Z359.3-2007, Safety Requirements for Positioning and Travel Restraint Systems.
- ANSI/ASSE Z359.4-2007, Safety Requirements for Assisted-Rescue and Self-Rescue Systems, Subsystems and Components.

Australian / New Zealand Safety Standards

- AS/NZS 1891.1:1995/Amdt 5:2004: Industrial fall-arrest systems and devices - Safety belts and harnesses.
- AS/NZS 1891.4:2000: Industrial fall-arrest systems and devices - Selection, use and maintenance.

Selection of Worker

Check: You have decided that the supervision/team leader should have known better than to select this particular worker or these particular team members because for some reason they were incapable of performing the work.

Ideas:

- You should continue investigating the problem until you can specify why the worker / team members were incapable of performing the work and how the supervisor/team leader could have detected and prevented this problem.

not qualified:

Check: You have decided that the worker made an error while performing the task because he was not fully qualified to perform the task.

Ideas:

- If you have a well-understood, generally well-used qualification program, then you should consider the reasons why, in this special case, the program was not used. You can then suggest corrective action to deal with this exception.

- If you don't have a well-understood and generally well-used qualification program that provides supervisors with guidelines or rules about who can perform what work, this is probably a generic problem and you should review the corrective action suggested below.

Ideas for Generic Problems:

- You should consider recommending the needed improvements from the following ideas (or other ideas that would solve your particular problem).

- First, consider developing qualification guidance for supervisors/ team leaders so that they would know what qualifications are required for particular jobs.

    a. This requires the development of:
       - job categories,
       - training and qualifications standards, and
       - continuing training requirements.
    b. Cross training can be used to provide a flexible work force.
    c. The guidance should specify what is to be done if qualified workers are not available and how to keep people qualified or get them requalified.

- Consider evaluating the workforce and the distribution of qualified workers to see if sufficient qualified workers are available to perform the expected workload. Also, consider evaluating the requirements for qualified workers for emergency or plant upset conditions.

    a. If this study highlights problems, consider redistributing the qualified workers or the workload.

- Next, consider implementing the qualification program and developing a list (paper or computer-based) of the personnel available and their qualifications.
    - If this is computer-based, the interface should make it easy for supervisors to sort by work type, qualification, and shift assignment so that the supervisor can easily identify who is available and qualified to perform a certain task.

- Consider providing training for the supervisors/team leaders and the workers on the qualification requirements and the qualification list.
    - The intent of the training is that the supervisors/team leaders and workers clearly understand who can perform what work, how to use

the qualification list, the potential problems that using unqualified workers can create, and what to do if no qualified workers are available or if there is disagreement about the qualification requirements.

- Once the guidance is in place and the training has been completed, you should consider recommending an audit program to see that the qualification guidance is being used properly.
  - The audits should reinforce (positive feedback) proper use of the guidelines and point out improvements that are needed.

References:

- Code of Federal Regulations (Pharmaceuticals) 21CFR211.25, *Personnel Qualifications*

fatigued:

Check: You have decided that the worker had difficulties when performing the task because he/she was not alert or not "thinking straight" due to working excessive overtime, working a second job, bad shift scheduling, sleep disorders, or other factors that would cause the worker to be fatigued.

Ideas:

- When you make your corrective action recommendation, you should consider addressing both the reasons for the fatigue and the reasons why the supervisor assigned a fatigued worker.

- Also, a major factor in selecting appropriate corrective actions is the difference between a specific fatigue problem and a generic fatigue problem. For example, a worker may suffer from sleep apnea. This breathing disorder causes the worker to have inadequate sleep at night. Because of this lack of proper sleep at night, the individual may instantly nod off at other times (maybe while working). The solution for the fatigue would be medical and oriented toward the individual. The solution for the supervisor might be training to recognize this type of problem. In a healthcare scheduling problem, doctors could be scheduled to work 36 hours on followed by 120 hours off. All doctors would be fatigued prior to the end of their 36 hour shift. Therefore, this would be a generic problem requiring a systemic change that would alter the work pattern for all doctors.

- Because the individual reasons for fatigue can be as varied as individuals, we will concentrate here on the generic reasons for fatigue and the detection of fatigue.

Ideas for Generic Problems:

- When you make your corrective action recommendation for correction of the generic problem, you should consider addressing both the reasons for the fatigue and the reasons why the supervisor/team leader assigned a fatigued worker. First we will discuss detection of the fatigue problem and then we will discuss prevention of fatigue.

  a. To help supervisors/team leaders recognize fatigue problems, you should consider providing training for the supervisor in recognizing fatigue and actions to take when workers become fatigued.

  b. You may also consider obtaining alertness assessment computer programs that test the worker to see if their performance is declining because of fatigue problems. Programs available include tests to see how fast the eye reacts to changes in the intensity of a light source and manual tracking tasks that measure motor skills and reaction times.

  c. You may also consider developing a program and training to teach people how to recognize and self-report fatigue. This would include what to do if they don't believe they have received adequate sleep or if they believe they are too fatigued to perform a particular job.

- You will also have to consider developing reasonable actions for the supervisor to take once excessive fatigue is detected. For example, if you tell the supervisor not to use fatigued workers but provide them with the requirement of running a continuous process, provide them with no "spare" employees, and provide no "relief" workers if a fatigued worker is detected, the supervisor has little or no choice but to use the fatigued worker. Therefore, you will have to consider if fatigue is a serious enough problem to recommend setting up a systematic process to assure a non-fatigue workforce.

- Next, you should consider developing actions to reduce the fatigue. These could include:

  a. Some fatigue problems are related to 24-hour work schedules (shift work). In these cases, optimizing the shift schedule may help reduce fatigue in workers. For more information about optimizing shift scheduling and addressing fatigue issues, see *The Twenty Four Hour Society*, (1993) by Dr. Martin Moore-Ede, published by Addison-Wesley Publishing Company, Reading, MA.

  b. Another factor in workers who face rotating work schedules can be how the worker eats and attempts to sleep. Research has shown that some "lifestyle" choices can reduce fatigue. Therefore, you may also consider developing a sleep education program to train workers in proper techniques to improve sleep when on shift work and some lifestyle ideas for reducing fatigue.

c. There is currently extensive research going on about sleep, sleep disorders, and fatigue. To get the latest information, you should probably consult the Internet to see if any recent research could impact the problem you are facing. See the references provided below for more ideas.

d. Some fatigue problems are related to excessive overtime. You may also consider developing policies that limit overtime on a job or restrict workers from working other jobs that prevent them from getting adequate rest, relaxation, and sleep.

The U.S. Nuclear Regulatory Commission has defined limits on work hours for nuclear plant workers in safety-critical jobs in Federal Regulations (10CFR26 subpart I). If you have workers whose performance is critical to safety, quality, or your company's financial well-being, you may want to recommend the adoption of these limits for your facility. The regulatory guidance is as follows:

"Licensees shall ensure that any individual's work hours do not exceed the following limits:

- 16 work hours in any 24-hour period;
- 26 work hours in any 48-hour period; and
- 72 work hours in any 7-day period.

"Licensees shall ensure that individuals have, at a minimum, the rest breaks specified as follows:

- A 10-hour break between successive work periods or an 8-hour break between successive work periods when a break of less than 10 hours is necessary to accommodate a crew's scheduled transition between work schedules or shifts AND
- A 34-hour break in any 9-day period.

"Licensees shall ensure that individuals have, at a minimum, the number of days off specified in this paragraph. For the purposes of this subpart, a day off is defined as a calendar day during which an individual does not start a work shift. For the purposes of calculating the average number of days off required in this paragraph, the duration of the shift cycle may not exceed 6 weeks.

- Individuals who are working 8-hour shift schedules shall have at least 1 day off per week, averaged over the shift cycle;
- Individuals who are working 10-hour shift schedules shall have at least 2 days off per week, averaged over the shift cycle;
- Individuals who are working 12-hour shift schedules shall have at least 2.5 days off per week, averaged over the shift cycle.

"During the first 60 days of a unit outage, licensees need not meet the requirements of this section while those individuals are working on unit outage activities. However, the licensee shall ensure that these individuals have at least 3 days off in each successive (i.e., non-rolling) 15-day period."

    e.   Another reason that people may be fatigued is that too much work is being scheduled in too short a period of time. If this is a problem, you may want to conduct a study to determine how much work should be assigned. See the references below for more information on how to conduct time and motion studies.

- If you decide to implement any new policy or requirements, you should consider how you will train all those affected by the change.

- You should also consider periodic audits for compliance with any new rule or policy that is made.

References:

For more information about optimizing shift scheduling and addressing fatigue issues, see:

- *The Twenty Four Hour Society*, (1993) by Dr. Martin Moore-Ede, published by Addison-Wesley Publishing Company, Reading, MA.

- *Making Shiftwork Tolerable*, (1992) by T. H. Monk and S. Folkard, published by Taylor and Francis, Pb: 0-85066-822-0.

- For more books and information about fatigue and shiftwork, go to the Circadian Technologies, Inc. website at: www.shiftwork.com.

- 10CFR26 Subpart I, Nuclear Regulatory Commission Fitness For Duty requirements.

For information about the latest sleep, fatigue, and shiftwork research, try these web sites:

- University of Illinois Clockworks: www.life.uiuc.edu

- Society for Light Treatment & Biological Rhythms: www.psychiatry.ubc.ca

- Society for Research on Biological Rhythms: www.srbr.org

- Center for Biological Timing: www.cbt.virginia.edu

- National Science Foundation: www.nsf.org

- American Medical Association: www.ama-assn.org

- NTSB / NASA Fatigue Resource Directory: http://olias.arc.nasa.gov/zteam/fredi/fredi.sec3.html

- Federal Aviation Administration: www.hf.faa.gov

To find out more about fatigue countermeasures see:

- NASA / FAA Fatigue Countermeasures Program: http://aerospace.nasa.gov/library/chicago/fcp.htm

- List of NASA's Fatigue Countermeasures Group publications: http://human-factors.arc.nasa.gov/zteam/fcp/FCP.pubs.html

- To find out more about software for testing workers for fitness for duty call 301-816-9212 or see www.pmifit.com.

- Fatigue Risk Management Systems: http://casa.gov.au/aoc/fatigue/

- Fatigue Risk Control Guide: www.worksafe.vic.gov.au/wps/wcm/resources/file/eb27484fe954483/fatigueriskcontrolguide.doc

- Center for Sleep Research: : http://www.unisa.edu.au/sleep/publications/default.asp

To find out more about time & motion studies to determine how much work can be assigned in a particular time period, consider reading:

- *Manprint, An Approach To Systems Integration,* (1990) Chapter 9, Workload Assessment & Prediction (pages 257 - 296) edited by Harold Booher, published by Van Nostrand Reinhold, New York, NY.

- *Handbook of Industrial Engineering,* Chapter 4.4 (1982), edited by Gavriel Salvendy, published by John Wiley & Sons, New York.

- *Motion and Time Studies,* 6th Edition (1976) by Ben W. Niebel, published by Irwin, Homewood, IL.

- *Motion and Time Study: Principles and Practices,* 5th Edition (1978) by Marvin Mundel, published by Prentice-Hall, Engelwood Cliffs, NJ.

- *Motion and Time Study: Design and Measurement of Work,* 7th Edition (1980) by Ralph Barnes, published by John Wiley & Sons, New York.

upset:

Check: You have decided that the worker had difficulties when performing the task because he was emotionally upset and that supervision should have detected this before assigning him.

Ideas:

- When you make your corrective action recommendation, you should consider addressing how you can assure that upset employees are not assigned to perform critical tasks that have a significant environmental, health, safety, quality, or production impact.

- You should also consider addressing why the supervisor was either unable to detect that the worker was upset or unwilling to assign another worker to perform the task.

- To learn more about identifying and reassigning upset employees, you should consider attending training on detection of aberrant behavior. Courses on this topic have been taught in the nuclear industry and the military. You could then conduct similar training for supervisors/team leaders to help them recognize upset employees and take appropriate action.

- You may also consider obtaining work performance assessment computer programs that test the worker to see if their performance is declining because of fatigue or substance abuse problems. Programs available include tests to see how fast the eye reacts to changes in the intensity of a light source and manual tracking tasks that measure motor skills and reaction times. Depending on the program, it may also be able to detect declines in the worker's performance because of emotional problems (consult with the program's developers for additional information).

- You may also consider developing a fitness for duty program to train workers to recognize problems, like being upset, so they can see how they can recognize the problem and self-report potential issues that their supervisor or the human relations department should be aware of. An example might be the serious illness or death of a spouse, conflicts on the job, or serious financial problems that distract the worker from performance of critical tasks.

- If the supervisor knowingly assigned a worker that was upset to perform critical work, you should consider corrective action that would address the reason the supervisor assigned that particular worker.
  - This could include training for the supervisor about the effects of emotional overload on task performance, the actions that supervisors/team leaders are supposed to take when an employee is upset and, in the opinion of the supervisor, potentially incapable of accurately and dependably performing the task.

- Once an aberrant behavior program has been established, you should consider recommending that people who voluntarily report problems or supervisors/team leaders that use the program are rewarded (not punished) for use of the program.
  - You would need to ensure that workers in the program are not discriminated against and that the supervisor's job is not made more difficult by using the program.

Ideas for Generic Problems:

- Hopefully, upset employees are NOT a generic problem. If they are, you have a serious human relations problem that needs serious management attention.

References:

- *Victims, Villains, and Heroes: Managing Emotions in the Workplace,* (2002) by Don Phin and Loy Young, published by Aquarius House.

Check: You have decided that the worker had difficulties when performing the task because he was impaired due to substance abuse problems, and the supervisor/team leader was aware or should have been aware of the problem.

Ideas:

- When you make your corrective action recommendation, you should consider addressing how you can assure that employees with performance problems due to substance abuse are not assigned to perform critical tasks that have a significant environmental, health, safety, quality, or production impact.

- You should also consider addressing why the supervisor/team leader was either unable to detect that the worker had substance abuse problems or unwilling to assign another worker to perform the task.

- To learn more about identifying and reassigning employees with substance abuse problems, you should consider attending training on detection of aberrant behavior. Courses on this topic have been taught in the nuclear industry and the military.

- To help supervisors/team leaders recognize employees with substance abuse problems, you should consider providing training for the supervisor in aberrant behavior and actions to take when the supervisor believes that the employee has a substance abuse problem.

- You may also consider obtaining work performance assessment computer programs that test the worker to see if their performance is declining because of substance abuse problems. Programs available include tests to see how fast the eye reacts to changes in the intensity of a light source and manual tracking tasks that measure motor skills and reaction times.

- You may also want to consider implementing a random drug and alcohol testing program. Many companies have found that these programs quickly weed out chronic substance abusers.

- You may also consider developing a fitness for duty program to train workers to recognize substance abuse problems so they can recognize the problem and report potential issues to their supervisor or the human relations department.

- When developing these recommendations, you should consider getting legal counsel and human relations professionals involved.
    - The Americans with Disabilities Act (ADA), other national standards or requirements, privacy laws, state laws, and other

factors need to be considered when developing policies that deal with substance abuse.

- If the supervisor knowingly assigned a worker that was drunk or on drugs to perform critical work, you should consider corrective action that would address the reason the supervisor assigned that particular worker. This could include disciplinary action for the supervisor and the employee.

- You should also consider providing training for supervisors/team leaders about the effects of substance abuse on task performance, the actions that supervisors/team leaders are supposed to take when an employee is suspected of substance abuse and, in the opinion of the supervisor, potentially incapable of accurately and dependably performing the task.
  - This training should include any legal precautions that need to be taken and the rights of the employee who is suspected to be a substance abuser.

- Once an aberrant behavior program has been established, you should consider recommending that people who voluntarily report problems or supervisors/team leaders that use the program are rewarded (not punished) for use of the program.
  a. You would need to ensure that workers who voluntarily self-report problems would then be assigned to some type of rehabilitation program.
  b. You would also have to ensure that participants are not discriminated against if their performance improves and they are able to rejoin the workforce and avoid future substance abuse problems.
  c. You should also ensure that the supervisor's job is not made more difficult by using the program.

- Again, consult your legal counsel and human relations professionals before implementing any corrective actions for substance abuse problems.

Ideas for Generic Problems:

- Hopefully, drunk and drugged employees are NOT a generic problem at your company.

References:

- To find out more about software for testing workers for fitness for duty call 301-816-9212 or see www.pmifit.com.

- 10CFR26, Nuclear Regulatory Commission standards on Fitness For Duty.

Work Direction (Selection of Worker)

- *Investigation of Substance Abuse in the Workplace,* (1990) by Peyton Schur and James Broder, published by Butterworth-Heinemann.

- OSHA's position on providing a drug-free workplace, (1998) http://www.osha.gov/pls/oshaweb/owadisp.show_document?p_table=INTERPRETATIONS&p_id=22577.

team selection NI:

Check: You have decided that the supervisor/team leader assigned the wrong mixture of expertise or experience or assigned team workers with pre-existing personal conflicts between them that kept them from working together effectively.

Ideas:

- When you make your corrective action recommendation, you should consider addressing how you can ensure that employees assigned to perform a task have the right mix of expertise and experience and don't have pre-existing personal conflicts that make cooperation unlikely. Special emphasis should be given to critical tasks that have a significant environmental, health, safety, quality, or production impact.

- You should also consider addressing why the supervisor either didn't know the workers had the wrong blend of skills or that they were unable to work together or why the supervisor/team leader was unwilling or unable to assign a different worker or workers to perform the task.

- To learn more about team performance and promoting better teamwork, you should consider attending a cockpit resource management or a crew teamwork training course to learn more about promoting teamwork. These courses have been given in the aviation industry for crew teamwork during flight and for maintenance of aircraft. They have also been given in the nuclear industry to promote shift teamwork.

- You may also consider developing a crew teamwork program to train workers to recognize and report crew teamwork problems so the problems can be corrected before accidents or incidents occur.

- If the supervisor/team leader knowingly assigned workers that didn't have the proper skills or were known to have interpersonal conflicts, you should also consider providing training for supervisor/team leader about the effects of teamwork problems on task performance, the actions that supervisor/team leader are supposed to take to ensure proper teamwork, and the potential disciplinary action that can be

Work Direction (Selection of Worker)

taken if a supervisor/team leader knowingly assigns people who are incapable of working together to perform a task.

    a.   In this case you may also consider the use of the discipline policies to punish unacceptable actions by the supervisor/team leader or the employees that were involved.

    b.   Of course, you should consider getting human relations or legal counsel's opinions before firing or disciplining an employee or a supervisor/team leader because of a team selection problem.

- Once crew teamwork training has been established, you should consider recommending that people who use the program are rewarded (not punished) for use of the program. You would need to follow through to see that workers and supervisors/team leaders who point out crew teamwork problems are rewarded.

Ideas for Generic Problems:

- Hopefully, assigning employees with pre-existing personality conflicts to perform work is NOT a generic problem at your company.

- However, if assigning people with the wrong mix of skills to perform the work is a generic problem, then you should consider recommending a study to determine what mix of skills is required for critical tasks that have a significant environmental, health, safety, quality, or production impact.

- Once you developed this information, you could then include staffing suggestions in your qualification program, your policies, or your procedures so that supervisors/team leaders would have a reference and rules to use to help make these decisions.

- Next, you would have to train the supervisors/team leaders in this information so that they could use it in when making work assignments.

- You should also consider recommending audits of the work assignments to see if the requirements are being followed.

References:

- *Cockpit Resource Management,* (1995) edited by Earl L. Wiener, Barbara G. Kanki, and Robert L. Helmreich, published by Academic Press, Orlando, FL.

- FAA standard: Cockpit resource management training (Advisory Circular No. 120-51), Federal Aviation Administration, Washington, DC.

- *The Industrial Operator's Handbook: A Systematic Approach to Industrial Operations,* (2001) by H.C. Howlett, Pocatello, ID: Techstar.

Supervision During Work	**Check:** You have decided that some type of supervisory problem during performance of the work contributed to the problem or could have prevented the problem but did not.

Ideas:

- You should continue to investigate the problem until you have identified a particular supervisory issue that contributed to the problem.

- You can then develop corrective action to address this supervisory issue.

- If you can't identify the particular supervisory issue involved but you believe that better supervision should have prevented the problem, consider performing a Safeguards Analysis (Chapter 10 of the *TapRooT® Book,* 2008) with special emphasis on the potential supervisory barriers to the problem. This may lead you to additional requirements for supervision of a particular task.

no supervision:

Check: You have decided that the problem would have been prevented by a reasonable level of supervision at the worksite or by the supervisor/team leader providing support, coverage, or oversight of the work.

Ideas:

- Your corrective action should address the particular supervisory problem that you identify.

- You should consider the need for training for the supervisor/team leader to communicate the expected supervisory responsibilities and actions to be taken for the type of work performed that was involved in the problem.

- If the supervisor/team leader has been trained, you may want to identify the specific reason why the supervisor/team leader failed to supervise the job even though he had been trained to do so.

Ideas for Generic Problems:

- If you haven't developed guidance and training for the supervisors/team leaders on their role in ensuring that work is performed correctly, you should consider developing training for them.
  a. To develop this training, you would need to assess the knowledge, skills, and abilities that are required of a supervisor/team leader and the proper role of the supervisor/team leader during performance of particular tasks.

b. You would then develop training for the supervisor/team leader and conduct post training assessments to make sure that the supervisors/team leaders learned the new skills.

- If the supervisor/team leader failed to supervise work that they normally would have supervised but they didn't have time to supervise it because of excessive workload, you should consider reducing the supervisor's workload (perhaps by developing some kind of automation that helps the supervisor/team leader be more efficient), reducing the amount of work being performed, or developing some kind of other supervisory presence to observe work in the field (assistant supervisors, work team leaders, senior workers, or self-directed teams).

- You may also consider recommending audits of particularly critical jobs (high risk) that require supervision to see if proper supervision is used.

- These are just a few possibilities. Of course, other possibilities exist to ensure proper supervision during work. You may want to get professional assistance or review industry best practices before completing the development of your corrective action for this Root Cause.

References:

- *The Industrial Operator's Handbook: A Systematic Approach to Industrial Operations,* (2001) by H.C. Howlett, Pocatello, ID: Techstar.

crew teamwork NI:

Check: You have decided that the problem was caused by or made worse by poor teamwork among the people performing the work.

Ideas and Ideas for Generic Problems:

- When you make your corrective action recommendation, you should consider addressing how you can ensure that both the supervisor/ team leader and the workers involved understand the importance of teamwork to reliable team performance and understand the techniques that they should use to ensure proper teamwork during the job.

- To learn more about team performance and promoting better teamwork, you should consider attending a cockpit resource management or a crew teamwork training course to learn more about promoting teamwork. These courses have been given in the aviation industry for crew teamwork during flight and for maintenance of aircraft. They have also been given in the nuclear industry to promote shift teamwork.

- Consider developing a crew teamwork program to train workers to be effective team members and to recognize and report crew teamwork problems so the problems can be corrected before accidents or incidents occur.

- Once crew teamwork training has been established, Consider recommending that people who use the program are rewarded (not punished) for use of the program. You would need to follow through to see that workers and supervisors/team leaders who point out crew teamwork problems are rewarded.

- Consider developing some type of management/expert crew teamwork audit program to assess the status of crew teamwork and to recommend ways to improve any crew teamwork programs that you have implemented.

- Consider developing supervisory displays that highlight overall mission requirements and help the supervisor/team leader maintain the "big picture" view of the system during emergencies or plant upsets.

References:

- *Cockpit Resource Management,* (1995) edited by Earl L. Wiener, Barbara G. Kanki, and Robert L. Helmreich, published by Academic Press, Orlando, FL.

- FAA standard: Cockpit resource management training (Advisory Circular No. 120-51), Federal Aviation Administration, Washington, DC.

Glossary

>	Greater Than
A & E	Audits and Evaluations
Admin	Administrative
Comm	Communication
CRT	Cathode Ray Tube
DCS	Distributed Control System
Equip	Equipment
ER	Equipment Room or Emergency Room
Hold Point	A step in a procedure that requires an inspection before the worker can move on to the next step. Therefore, at that point they "hold" or wait for the inspection to be completed.
LTA	Less Than Adequate
MOC	Management of Change
NI	Needs Improvement
PdM	Predictive Maintenance
PIO	Potential Improvement Opportunity
PM	Preventive or Predictive Maintenance
QC	Quality Control
QV	Quality Verification
RBI	Risk-Based Inspection
RCM	Reliability-Centered Maintenance
SPAC	Standards, Policies, or Administrative Controls
Specs	Specifications
Typo	Typographical Error

SMARTER Matrix

Use the Corrective Action Helper® module to develop a specific fix.

Causal Factor:
Root Cause:
SPECIFIC: In detail, describe the corrective action or actions needed to fix the root cause (See the Corrective Action Helper® for ideas): Are specific policies/procedures/training/tools/PPE/etc. or special conditions needed to implement this corrective action?
MEASURABLE: How will you verify that the corrective action was completed as intended? (Verification): Who will verify and by what date?
ACCOUNTABLE: Who will be responsible for implementing the fix and do they have the authority and resources they need?
REASONABLE: What is the business case for this improvement? What is Return On Investment (ROI) or Cost Benefit Ratio of this fix? What are the likely consequences if this fix IS NOT implemented?
TIMELY: What is a reasonable time to implement the fix? Are temporary actions needed before the fix is completed to ensure safety, quality, production, or environmental responsibility? (Yes/No) If so, describe these temporary actions:
EFFECTIVE: How will the fix eliminate the root cause and prevent recurrence of the Causal Factor? Will the fix continue to be effective in years to come? How will you measure the effectiveness after implementation? (Validation) Who will measure the effectiveness and by what date?
REVIEWED: Has the fix been independently reviewed for unintended consequences by those that will be impacted and by maintenance, engineering, safety / quality / environmental oversight, or others? Does this fix cause any new risks that need to be addressed? (Yes/No) Document the review:

Attach additional pages if needed